HOW TO GET OUT OF 1
The Ultimate Self Em

As long as there is death, there is fear.
Only victory over death will make fear die.

Copyright 2000 – 2012

Version 5.0

ISBN 978-0615658582

© Photography from Michel Fraile
© Translation from French into English by Antoine Laurent and Alain Forget 2012.

To my Teachers: René Ropars and Jean Tissier.
For years they helped me to go forward, allowing me to stumble but never to fall.
To Terence Gray (Wei Wu Wei), contemporary Ch'an Master through whose texts awakening occurred.

TABLE OF CONTENTS

PART III

BIOGRAPHIES AND SELECTED TEXTS

ACKNOWLEDGEMENTS

I would like to thank Dr Leon Schlamm, Dr. Richard Dixey, Geoffrey Russell, Catherine Phillips, Mark Lloyd-Fox, Barry Tomalin, Mary Tomalin, Michael Laznicka and the late Colin Morley for their invaluable contributions to the revision of this text.

I also wish to show my appreciation to Dr. Donald Wilson, Jacques Renault, Victoria Ritchie, Monique Sims and Alex Tschyrkow for their critical reading.

I am grateful for the help given over the years to the development of the Teaching by Gérard Galbois, Laurence Kirschel, Micha Benoliel, John Cummins, Dr. Jérome Bilet, Dr Elisabeth Doeskeland, Isabelle Clerc, Mattie Silman, David Lorimer, Dr Peter Fenwick, Elisabeth Fenwick and Viviane Auberton.

And, finally, I am grateful for the comments and suggestions I received from Dr Mark Collins, Charlie Savill and from my translator and close collaborator, Dr. Antoine Laurent.

FOREWORD: DR MARK COLLINS

I first met Alain Forget in 2003, little knowing that the meeting would have such a profound impact on my life. At the time I was, and indeed still am, a busy psychiatrist practising in London. My daily work involves listening to people talking about themselves, their fears, their guilt, the things that made them feel bad. You might identify addictive behaviors, dysfunctional relationships, unhealed wounds from the past or any number of things that lead to people being stuck in a repetitive cycle of pain. Mine are the conventional tools of psychiatry and I would seek to help people through therapy, medication and sometimes hospitalisation.

I have always been open to a more holistic approach and am happy to work with some alternative practitioners, but the 'spiritual' side of things was seldom an avenue that I explored. It is only more recently that I have realized that the patient lying on the couch and the monk sitting in a cave in the Himalayas are essentially seeking the same thing.

My own background includes a moderately conventional English upbringing, my father, a clergyman, always emphasizing that his Christian faith was based on doubt, or it would not be faith but certainty. As a late teenager (in the 1960's) I was introduced to Eastern religions and philosophies, and spent a year travelling in India. There seemed to be something more alive, a more profound resonance within me provoked by what I read and studied in a somewhat dilettanteish way. Metaphysical questions presented themselves, but were then overtaken by life as my ego sought to define its existence more clearly.

The next several decades were the usual roller-coaster of experiences, some happy, some sad, successes and failures, relationships forged and broken, that represent my life history. From time to time the metaphysical questions would resurface, often after painful episodes, only to be forgotten again as I set about unconsciously repeating the same old patterns. Occasionally, in a moment of clarity, I would recognize that inside I had not fundamentally changed since childhood, and that various very basic emotions, such as fear, were driving me.

This was the backdrop against which I met Alain Forget. Out of politeness to a friend I went reluctantly to a talk he was giving, with no idea of what to expect. His talk was a distillation of the contents of this book and it engaged me intellectually. There was simultaneously an excitement generated by the clarity, simplicity yet profundity of what I was hearing, along with a critical dialogue in my head about those things with which I disagreed or thought to be nonsense. The closer it came to 'my' territory of psychology, the more I challenged what I heard.

At the same time I was reacting strongly at a non-verbal level, and during a period in the talk when Alain sat in silence, along with the thirty or so people in the room listening to him, I experienced something extraordinary. There was an array of very specific sensory, particularly visual, phenomena, linked to an emotional cascade which was hugely powerful and remarkable, especially for not having been at all anticipated, and also for the fact that I was simultaneously able to observe myself having the experience. I later learned that my experience was a common one, and Alain describes the phenomena in a very matter-of-fact way in his book. Without a doubt it changed the course of my life irrevocably.

Since then I have tried to meet Alain each month when he visits London, and have sought to follow his advice. This has been an extremely interesting experience, not the least for the observations of the ways in which I have resisted change. An earlier version of this book simply entitled 'The Four Ds', was dutifully read by me and then subjected to critical analysis. Perhaps, I thought, I could correct Alain on the more obvious mistakes he had made in the psychological sections of the book. I am reasonably intelligent, and pride myself on having a particularly good memory, so was surprised to find that on each meeting with Alain I invariably failed to remember what all four of the Ds stood for. I could usually manage three but never all four even if I did a spot of quick revision just before the meeting.

When I finally confessed my amnesia, Alain roared with laughter and indicated that his French students, whom he had been teaching for considerably longer, often had the same problem. I had experienced my first encounter with the awesome power of the ego in defending itself when under attack. Not for nothing does Alain's surname mean what it does when pronounced in the English manner!

In similar fashion, I had a huge problem with Alain linking the development of guilt with the pain of birth. I read and re-read the passages about this, becoming more and more indignant each month, arguing with Alain, and reaching a point where I seriously considered discontinuing seeing him. Needless to say, in a moment of catharsis, I was able to see clearly that my protestations were based on denial of my own core of guilt. This process has repeated itself frequently, but fortunately Alain is a patient teacher.

Many of us may have been fortunate enough in our school-days to have been taught by a particularly inspiring teacher who was able to bring a subject to life. Alain Forget has, in my experience, an ability to do this in the most important subject there is, namely our very existence, or lack of it! By practising the Four Ds and following the suggestions and understanding the teachings outlined in the book, I have moved further and faster than I was able to over the years in my conventional therapy. The way I work professionally has also changed.

This book, as Alain says, is a map. It provides clear instructions on what to do and where to go. Reading it and re-reading it has for me been an illuminating experience, one which I hope may bring as much pleasure and growth to others as it has to me.

Mark Collins
MA MB BS MRCP MRCPsych
London.

FOREWORD: DR PETER FENWICK

For millennia humans have sought to find out who they are, what is their place in the cosmos and how they can achieve their full potential as individuals. Some teachers have become fully awakened and it is the achievement of this state that is the growing point of spiritual evolution.

Alain Forget is one of the leaders of a new wave of philosophers who, through working on themselves, using the tools bequeathed to us by the ancient Masters, have achieved a breakthrough in his experience of consciousness.

A teacher can only teach when he understands the subject. The development of a wider state of consciousness is not something you understand. It is something that is experienced only after many years of practice and hard work on yourself.

Many of the early teachers had the same goals as Alain – an awakened state of consciousness – but their teachings come to us from different cultures and their words have different and subtle shades of meaning that are not easily accessible to their translators or to those of us from a Western culture who try to follow their methods to reach the same goals. Alain's achievement is to use the language of today and to have devised a psychological method that immediately appeals to us, that is easy to understand and that is very effective.

His method is practical and involves a graded series of strategies which, if practised sincerely and intensively, leads to understanding and, finally, to the dissolution of the ego.

He points out that the ego is mechanical and that the only thing we can do is to train a part of the ego to work on the ego.

He reminds us that everything that we do or say or think is a manifestation of the ego.

The goal is the ego-less state. He clearly explains that deep metaphysical questioning combined with psychological introspection can achieve that.

His method, the Four Ds, is a method for the 21st century. It is easy to understand and easy to apply.

Distancing – non-reactive attentiveness – Discernment – psychological introspection – Disidentification – the letting go which is the result of the two – and Discrimination – deep metaphysical self-questioning – are the steps that you must climb to loosen the ego and, finally, make it see that it is not.

I cannot recommend this method too highly. It requires no guru, just continual understanding and practice. Every time any thought comes into the mind, it is an opportunity for growth.

Dr Peter Fenwick
MB Bsc BChir FRCPsych
London.

A SHORT DESCRIPTION OF MY JOURNEY

Awakening occurred one afternoon in the winter of 1977–1978 in the half-light of the 12th century Gothic cathedral of Chartres. I would travel every day to this beautiful medieval town that lies about an hour away from Paris, where I would settle down to read certain metaphysical texts. I would then meditate for an hour and return home.

After three months of regular practice, while sitting in silence in the cathedral, a powerful question propelled me to a level beyond my mind. I suddenly saw that I was not my thoughts, not my emotions, not my psychological entity. For the first time, I had living proof of what the classical texts had been saying.

What that experience showed me is that awakening is nothing more than our natural state. It is always there, if masked by our psychological entity. An awakened person perceives people and things like everybody else, but he has lost his conditioning and has attained a state that is at one with life. Only that state is free of fear.

The system explained in this book has emerged from the work that I have undertaken on myself and is the result of a journey that I would like to share with you.

At the age of 20, the metaphysical questions that had preoccupied me during adolescence encouraged me to do further research. This eventually led me to the conclusion that there are parallels between the major spiritual, religious and philosophical traditions.

At the age of 22, I met my first teacher, a homeopathic doctor who had been one of Gurdjieff's students. From that moment I dedicated most of my spare time to becoming better acquainted with the philosophy of non-duality – Advaita Vedanta, the Ch'an Buddhist Masters, the Sufis and the Christian mystics.

At the age of 25, I had my first awakening in Chartres. My work over the next few years became more and more intense. I sat in silence in such remarkable places as the cathedral of Notre Dame in Paris, the Basilica in Santiago de Compostella and by the Wailing Wall in Jerusalem.

When I was 34, I met my second teacher, an elderly French-man who had been brought up by a Tibetan monk. The techniques that he taught me accelerated the development of my soul.

At the age of 39, the processes of this inner evolution intensified to such an extent that the ability to fuse with the states of unity or awakening became more and more frequent. Once I had experienced this opening up of consciousness, I understood that philosophers and mystics should not be considered as the representatives of their system of belief but as scientists who integrated or explored the state of higher consciousness. They are the scouts of our potential evolution.

In the next few years, I began to take notes on the techniques that had brought about awakening. My first students came from my circle of friends and acquaintances. They helped me to perfect the system that I call the philosophy of the 4Ds, a practical synthesis linked to my own experience that parallels those of the mystics. I next gathered together a number of people in London and in New York whom I see on a regular basis. I noticed over the course of the years that I could help them attain a state of consciousness that transcends time and space and transmit an energy that has the power to accelerate their evolution. I have also confirmed that as long as my students apply the right techniques, a new aspect will develop in them which will steer them towards a much more happy and successful life.

Monaco, January 2012

HOW THIS BOOK GOT ITS TITLE

The original title was 'The Philosophy of the 4Ds' but I felt it was a little too dry. Then, one day, I heard a Hank Williams' song and realized I had an idea for the title.

In his song, which is funny and downbeat, Hank tells us that he will never get out of this world alive. My own experience led me to the opposite conclusion which is why I have named my book 'How to Get out of this World Alive.' Its general theme is to reach the next level of our conscious evolution, build a body of light and energy and reach awakening.

It describes step-by-step how to get a clear understanding of how we function and how we can operate more effectively in the world.

So I'm pleased to say that Hank Williams was wrong and that if we 'struggle and strive' we can get out of this world alive.

INTRODUCTION

This book will help you to sharpen your questioning skills. And by asking yourself key questions such as "Who am I?", "What is the meaning of life?", "What is the origin of the universe?", you will feel more alive.

To get out of this world alive, you need to have a better understanding of who you are. The only elements that you have at hand are your thoughts, your emotions, your sensory perceptions and your dreams. Use them correctly and you will change your life.

This inner journey will be accomplished in four stages.

Distancing, the first stage, allows you to remain conscious of the thousands of thoughts and feelings that arise within you every day. To that end it makes full use of the body's sensations. Distancing is a technique and, like all techniques, it requires a period of learning and training. It shows you how mechanical you are. It allows you to see the automatic behavior patterns that rule you and to grasp how dominated those thoughts and feelings are by fear. It will also allow you to see the extent to which you repeat the same patterns and scenarios, a process easy to spot in others but much harder to acknowledge in yourself.

Through **Discernment**, the second D, you set up a method for introspection that will enable you to dig into the repressed unconscious layers you are made of and to dismantle your old sufferings. Soon, by applying the first two Ds, you will create a seeker* within yourself who will work for you on a permanent basis.

It is at this stage that your life starts to change for you identify less with fear and guilt. Thereafter the choices you make are better because they obey a different logic. As you begin to understand how you function, you gradually shift from making unconscious losing choices* to making conscious winning ones.

When you get to the third D, **Disidentification**, your evolution really accelerates. By letting go of your old patterns, you experience a finer quality of mental silence. If you then commit yourself to a consistent practice of introspection and silence, as many traditions have taught, you develop a psychic body, a soul that operates above thought, above memory. Other worlds open up to you. Although fear and guilt are still present, you are more and more on top of them. By moving above your shadow, above the undisclosed, repressed, fearful aspects of yourself, a new part of you made of light and energy connects to other dimensions.

The Fourth D, **Discrimination**, will permit you to abandon your final identification, the basic conditioning of you as a person that you have maintained all your life. You now discriminate between what you will become – Truth, the Absolute, consciousness of life itself, the Divine – and what you are about to surrender, your shadow, your repressed emotional body, that you have partly understood and dismantled through the practice of Distancing and Discernment. You will question the essence of the human condition: being, perception, who you are, who perceives? Once you have developed a taste for metaphysical inquiry, for deep questioning, at a certain moment one of these questions will lead you to your absence, to your emptiness. This disappearance of your mechanical nature is what Buddhists call the void, what Christians call the 'death of the old man'. Opening onto the void, causing the death of the old man are the means by which you can be born to awakening, to enlightenment, to Truth, to the Kingdom of Heaven. To reach this dimension is to encounter the freedom that you are seeking.

The reason why this text includes many quotations of spiritual teachers is because they are pioneers of consciousness. It is not the religions from which they came or founded that are of interest for religions are mere frameworks and systems of belief. What defines these teachers is that they take consciousness beyond frameworks and systems of belief, beyond everything with which you readily identify. In their wish to share this consciousness, they often disturbed the status quo and, like Jesus, Hallaj, Marguerite Porète and Socrates, paid the ultimate price.

Is it not extraordinary that, in spite of the thousands of years and thousands of miles that separate them, Christians such as Meister Eckhart, Sufis such as Hallaj, Hinduists such as Shankara, Taoists such as Lieh Tzu, Ch'an teachers such as Huang Po and many others deploy similar concepts and point towards a freedom beyond context and culture, beyond what conditions you? A freedom in which the observer dissolves in the observed. Spiritual teachers should not be thought of as representatives of systems of belief but as scientists who explored the upper levels of consciousness. As such, they are the scouts of man's ultimate frontiers. Is it not striking that quantum physics shows that the act of observation alters the very nature of what is being observed? And is it not remarkable that the Zohar, Lao Tzu and Jesus taught that you must balance your masculine and feminine sides? For what physics and psychology have discovered and put within easy reach, they stated hundreds, if not thousands of years ago.

Those who aspire to wisdom will soon develop the intuition that the One, the Absolute, lies at the origin of everything that we know. That sense of unity must be the point of departure for your search.

The Four Ds, whose principles have been known by different names in a variety of traditions, incorporate a method of self-inquiry that opens onto your true nature. One day it will suddenly appear beyond the constraints of polar opposites, beyond large/small, pleasure/pain, heaven/earth, being/non-being. It is what you really are. Once you realize this, you get out of this world alive for you are now beyond the polar opposites conscious/unconscious and are pure consciousness.

Whoever steps onto this path will encounter rapid results straightaway. Progress will depend on four qualities: a good level of awareness, willpower, courage and intellectual honesty. The more you intensify your practice, the more conscious you become, the more life reacts positively.

You can only be free if you know yourself. To achieve this, you must have the discipline and the courage to explore your foundations. It is only by applying the right techniques that you can first understand, then see, and at long last let go of the resistance covering up your fears and your guilt.

Myths and folk tales often tell the same story. A knight clad in armour – the ego – rides deep in the dark forest – the unconscious. His task is to vanquish dragons and demons – his guilt, his fears, his conflicts. On setting foot in the castle, he removes his armour and embraces the Sleeping Beauty lying in a glass coffin who instantly wakes up. This scene represents the union with your true nature.

This book is a manual which will guide you through life and towards its ultimate conscious state, awakening. It is designed to help you to ask questions about your motivations, your mechanisms, in other words yourself. To achieve the best results, you must obey two rules:

- You must have a real desire to change your life.

- You must accept that everything that happens to you happens because of you.

Unless these rules are taken seriously, you will not have the discipline to pursue the work on yourself and will blame others – your parents, your environment, society or God – for the troubles you face. Consequently you will never dig deep enough to explore your conditionings, nor dismantle the fear and guilt that lie at the root of your choices. At the same time it is important to be logical and coherent: although you induce what happens to you, if a disaster hits you, you are not responsible for the disaster, only for the way that you deal with it.

In this book the wisdom of the philosophers and mystics of the great traditions has been synthesized and adapted for today. You will discover, for example, that the concept of the sub-personalities was first elaborated by the Emperor Marcus Aurelius in the 2nd century AD. You will encounter a simple method of psychological introspection whose roots lie in Hinduism. You will learn to interpret and use your dreams in order to accelerate your evolution through an original and precise method that has proven its worth. The techniques that are found in various ancient texts have been brought together, tested and adapted for you in this practical manual.

This book provides a precise plan of the mechanisms of fear and guilt which run your life and explains how you can free yourself from them. It is divided in three parts. The first explains how your function, then develops the system of the 4Ds. The second is made up of the Questions and Answers that arose from a series of lectures given in London and New York between 2005–2012. The third, an anthology of the non-dualistic literature that lies at the base of the philosophy, includes quotations from the teachers of the principal traditions. There is also a glossary defining the core concepts, an extensive bibliography and a list of aphorisms.

PART I
THE FOUR DS

CHAPTER I

THE TWO KEYS AND THE FOUR MAPS

As we begin the practical work of exploring ourself, we need to understand what we are dealing with. To that end, we will make use of two keys and four maps. The more we use these keys, the greater will be our opportunity to open the doors that lead to freedom. The maps will help us locate ourself on our inner journey.

To make progress in the knowledge of ourself, it is essential to develop an understanding of Identification and Duality.

THE FIRST KEY: IDENTIFICATION

We identify all the time; with our gender: I am a man, I am a woman; with our appearance: I am tall or small, slim or fat. We identify with our state of health: I am well, I am ill; with our social status: I am rich, I am poor; with our nation, with our race, with our profession, with our belief system. This identification with what we think ourself to be shapes us as a person, as a psychological entity. We are infused with unconscious identifications which drive our successes and failures, making us strong, making us weak. To raise our level of consciousness means to disidentify bit by bit from everything with which we have identified. And, of course, as we dismantle the identifications that do not make us happy, that prevent us from reaching our full potential, our life will change for the better.

THE SECOND KEY: DUALITY

Duality is made up of the division between two opposites: big and small, hot and cold, good and evil. You are in duality because there is a division between you and what is not you.

Your identity can only exist if there is you on the one hand and the world on the other. Duality maintains itself through identification: I am this, I am that. Your identity, you as a person, will do everything it can to maintain the duality of which it is made. It will do so mechanically through identification with thought, with desire, with emotions and with sensory perceptions.

To help you understand what is duality, take the example of a wave and the ocean. Let us imagine that you are the wave. There is you, the wave, and there is the ocean. You are identified with your identity as a wave – warm or cold, big or small. The moment you realise that you are not the wave but the ocean, you are no longer in duality.

To work on yourself will consist in letting go of your identifications until your ego dissolves in unity just as the wave dissolves in the ocean. Only then will you transcend duality, only then will we get out of this world alive.

"Duality is at the root of all suffering."
Ashtavakra Gita. circa XIII–VIth century BC.

As you read this book, your understanding of identification and of duality will evolve.

THE FIRST MAP: FEAR AND GUILT
How they became linked and why they control our lives

Everything begins with birth.

The unborn child in its mother's womb is at one with its environment. It knows nothing else except its environment.

Floating happily in amniotic unity, the child is suddenly projected out of its original space. The shock of birth separates it from this initial environment and it experiences pain to come into the world.

From this shock, from this pain, comes the first identification between itself and the world.

There is the child on one side and its new environment on the other. There is the child and its encounter with pain. It is from this first pain that the mechanism of identification arises.

Identifying with the pain that it feels, the child becomes the vulnerable child*. The seed of fear and guilt has been planted.

The mechanism of identification will constitute our ego, and its function will be to protect the vulnerable child. The ego is built on the first identification with the pain linked to the process of birth. This pain, the first experience of our life, our first identification, will be at the origin of fear. This fear will be the ground on which guilt will form.

The first map shows us how fear and guilt appear to be the most appropriate concepts to define the adverse effects on our life of this identification with the pain of birth. It is only if we develop a clear comprehension of how these two forces condition us that we can begin to work on ourself, and this will radically change our life for the better.

Fear and guilt are closely linked. Fear is one of our constituent parts just as it is for all mammals. But the mixture of fear and guilt is characteristic of humans. We are aware of fear and manage it all the time. Guilt, however, is much less visible as it hides in the depths of our unconscious.

But if we take a look at the systems of belief that we have developed, we can see its presence.

The Judaic, Christian and Islamic religions are founded on the same myth. In the Old Testament God warns Adam: "You shall not eat of the tree of the Knowledge of Good and Evil for in the day that you eat of it you shall die." These religions are built on the guilt of having eaten the forbidden fruit. To have the Knowledge of Good and Evil means to enter duality. It means entering a dynamic in which the subject identifies with the object, the observer with the observed, the knower with the object known, and the first object of knowledge is the pain of birth.

The concept of original sin for Christians and of the Fall for Jews have as their origin the first pain that happens to us and, through identification, because of us.

In the major monotheistic systems of belief – Judaism, Christianity and Islam – guilt will be reinforced in the unconscious and in society through the concept of a transcendent God who rewards and punishes us through heaven or hell. This all-demanding God transmits laws via his prophets, via His Only Son sent as a sacrifice to redeem our sins, or via his Last Prophet, laws that everyone to a greater or lesser extent then breaks. These systems of belief will act as the collective logic that upholds our identification with guilt and which, like any identification, will attempt to maintain itself.

Fear and guilt are linked and feed each other. Established religions have for centuries employed both to keep their hold on power. Guilt also appears in the Asiatic systems of belief, be it Hinduism or Buddhism, through the concept of Karma, which explains that anything negative that happens in our life is the result of negative acts committed in past lives.

Education imposes limits and constraints. It is through this training that guilt will take shape and begin to appear at the conscious level.

The first effects of the connection between guilt and identification can be seen when a child of two or three identifies with a

* See Glossary

negative event that has occurred around him and with which he is in no way linked. For instance, when a child cries near him, he too will begin to cry, or when an object is broken, he will insist that he was not responsible. If years later the parents fight among themselves, the child will mechanically feel guilty. And if subsequently the parents divorce, the child will blame himself for this separation and will take upon himself the burden of guilt.

It is important to grasp that both the fear linked to the pain of birth and the guilt that will develop will be repressed by the unconscious. It will bury it as deeply as possible for that is how it functions. Guilt and fear represent the foundation upon which the unconscious is built and its task is to protect the vulnerable child. This vulnerability stems from identification with the pain of birth, with the shock of the first breath that burns the lungs and with the light that blinds the eyes. When Krishnamurti writes:

"But behind, the inevitable suffering hides away. One can evade it, try to forget it but it is always there. It cannot be denied and remains a deep wound which nothing seems to heal."

he is clearly aware of this reality.

To protect us from this suffering, the unconscious will develop layers, forming an armour. These layers will reinforce themselves by always returning to the same identifications to thoughts, desires, emotions and perceptions, to what can be called the same grabbing points.*

This is why throughout our life we keep reproducing the same scenarios. The different elements that make up our armour emerge into the light of consciousness to sustain or to renew their identifications. This logic which, stemming from the past, short-circuits the present, will make us experience again and again the same kind of success or failure in our emotional life, or in our financial affairs. This interaction between conscious and unconscious functions in a wholly mechanical manner. It is to maintain guilt and fear that we suffer from low self-esteem, from abandonment, from rejection and from repetitive failures. Guilt lies at the root of the self-limiting, sabotaging and self-destructive behavior that we encounter in our life. That explains why alcohol and drug abuse, which will inevitably trigger losing choices, will uphold and refuel the basic layers on which we are built.

When we are successful, it is always the result of a well-regulated compensation, that is to say we have become unified in a project that we bring to a conclusion by keeping ourself above our fears and guilt. In this case the unconscious losing choices that come from self-sabotaging layers have no hold on us.

The observation and dismantling of our automatic behavior patterns will become the very essence of the work on ourselves.

Our ego only exists in duality. It must maintain the subject-object dynamic to hold onto its identifications. These grabbing points are essential for its existence. If it loses them, it must create new ones at all cost. The Hydra, the Greek mythological monster with multiple heads, that when cut would immediately grow more, illustrates the ego and the logic it uses to maintain identification.

By developing a certain quality of observation, we will sense the presence of guilt behind the layers of which we are made for it engenders an illogical response in relation to the situation in which we find ourself. Consider the phenomenon of survivors' guilt. It is illogical that the survivor of a group that was almost wiped out should feel guilty. He should on the contrary feel overjoyed at being alive. So why does he feel guilty? Because the traumatic event – the tsunami, Auschwitz, the battlefield – has dismantled a portion of his identifications. The basic layer made of guilt will then mechanically emerge towards the conscious level to reinforce the identifications of the ego structure that is at risk of falling apart. We all remember the New York fireman on September 11th who said that he felt so guilty that his colleagues had died.

It is illogical that a child of ten or twelve should feel guilty about his parent's divorce. And it is equally illogical that the child brought up in a family where the parents are violent toward each other blames himself for that violence. It is illogical that the child of three identifies with a negative event to which he is not linked. The ego always activates its repressed structure when it loses part of its identifications or when they are at risk. **For the task of the ego is never to let go of its identifications.** It must protect at all cost the duality on which it depends for its survival by upholding the subject-object dynamic. To that end, just as the mythological Hydra regrows heads to survive, the ego will use guilt to reinforce or to replace identifications whenever they lose their grip.

If we look carefully, we may sense the presence of guilt behind our layers for it creates fear unrelated to the situation in which we find ourself. We all know people who are prone to irrational fears.

We should observe them to try to understand the origins of their fears. We will soon see that they have constructed a logic of guilt which both supports and stimulates fear. Fear always reinforces guilt and guilt activates fear. If we identify our guilt and recognize it as such, fear diminishes.

IN SUMMARY

- Our ego is made up of identifications.

- The first identification is the pain that we encounter during birth.

- The best available concepts to describe the effects on our lives of this first identification are fear and guilt.

- Guilt will develop through the pressures imposed by education.

- Guilt maintains itself through the systems of belief that we have developed.

- Guilt defines the repressed energy at the base of our losing choices.

- Guilt comes out in a mechanical and illogical manner to maintain our grabbing points whenever they let go.

- We can detect guilt when we see that it activates fear.

- Fear and guilt reinforce each other mutually.

THE SECOND MAP:
THE MAIN STRUCTURE OF THE EGO
or how we operate mechanically

The ego – we as a person, our psychological entity – is the result of human evolution. It divides into the conscious and unconscious. In order to manage its identifications, it operates in a purely mechanical manner using three programs.

At the deepest level of the ego is the first identification with the pain of birth, which will later turn into fear, then into guilt. It is the primary founding layer of the ego, the one that supports all the others. It is the base of the unconscious and the bedrock which holds up our psychological identity. The primary function of this identity is to protect the vulnerable child so that it can deal with the conflicts of existence. It is the armour that protects us from the violence of the world.

Within this first layer, evolution has set up a program whose task is never to let go of identification for duality must be maintained at any cost. That is why the psychological entity will always produce identifications which will feed fear and guilt in order to maintain its basic structure.

Where the conscious and the unconscious meet, there is another program which we share with all mammals and whose function is always to go towards the pleasant and to avoid the unpleasant. This program lies at the root of our inability to challenge ourselves as challenging ourselves is unpleasant. It is also responsible for our flights towards the pleasant, towards compensatory behavior. This explains why our society has built itself as a market-led society that offers us a series of infinite compensations.

These two programs have different tasks. On the one hand, a program protects the base that is made up of fear and guilt – a base that must never let go – and on the other hand, at the surface level, the other program goes towards the pleasant and avoids the unpleasant.

Faced by this contradiction, an intermediary program, a compromise program has evolved that strikes a balance between the other two – the choice of least harm. It is there to protect us according to the particular logic of our own history. We are all stuck at this level. In our love life and in our relationship to money, the same old patterns will tend to be reproduced again and again as they are the choice of least harm for us.

It is the choice of least harm that creates the repetitive situations such as success or ruin, health or sickness, riches or poverty that punctuate our lives.

Let us take the example of John, a thirty-five year old single man, whose shyness has consistently blocked him whenever he has wanted a relationship. He always finds reasons not to speak to any woman to whom he is attracted. For him, shyness represents the choice of least harm. It serves the purpose of preventing him from experiencing fear of rejection. Once he understands this, fear of rejection takes over as the new choice of least harm. As a result his shyness diminishes. When you identify a lower level, the one above it inevitably loses its power. The question that John should now put to himself is: 'What lies below my fear of rejection?' If he looks at what lies below it, he finds low self-esteem. As soon as he becomes conscious of that, he will be able to talk with greater freedom to a woman he finds attractive. And if he continues to question himself, he will discover guilt behind his low self-esteem.

The first advantage of working on oneself is that it raises the level of the choice of least harm. By changing what appears at the conscious level, we open ourselves to many more choices.

Our ego consists of layers and these make up our armour. Each layer has a task: to protect the one below it. It is because John began a process of introspection that he was able to dismantle the layers of shyness and of the fear of rejection.

IN SUMMARY

- The ego is the armour with which we face the world.

- This armour is managed by three defensive programs,
  or protective strategies.

  - A basic program: never let go of one's identifications.

  - A surface program: go towards the pleasant and
    avoid the unpleasant.

  - And an intermediary program, a compromise between the
    other two: the choice of least harm.

- The choice of least harm lies at the base of the repetitive situations that we encounter.

- By changing the choice of least harm, we change our live

> Man is the most violent species on this planet with regard to himself and to all other living creatures, which is why he dominates it. No other species turns upon itself as man does. To cope with this violence and to protect our vulnerable child, we need an armour. This armour, our ego, is made up of several layers managed by three programs.
>
> The more courage we can summon to dig into the primary causes of our behavior, the more our level of consciousness will rise. By raising our level of consciousness, we change the choice of least harm. To change our lives, we need to recognise the causes that lie at the origin of the choices that we make. Once the causes are recognized, they lose their power over us.

THE THIRD MAP:
THE ORIGINS OF THE SUBPERSONALITIES
or how our subpersonalities are shaped

We have seen how the first identification with pain occurs at birth and how it will be transformed into fear and guilt.

Much about the way we function is determined by what happens at this moment and over the next few years. Our recurrent dysfunctional patterns can be traced back to events which took place very early on in our development.

Our internal logic has been built essentially on three programs. The one that lies deepest in our unconscious is fear linked to identification with the pain of birth; the one on the surface is to go towards the pleasant and avoid the unpleasant; and the one in the middle is the choice of least harm, a compromise between the other two.

We now know that the brain is not a fixed structure with a predetermined shape, but that it grows and develops in response to interactions with the environment.

We can use the analogy of an oak tree. Although the acorn will determine the general nature of the grown tree, the particular shape of a tree will be influenced by the interplay of sunlight, wind, the quality of the soil and so on, which will all have an effect on its growth.

The brain, composed of billions of interconnecting nerve cells, grows somewhat like a tree, branching and rebranching, some limbs and twigs being favoured, others atrophying and becoming stunted.

Events that occur at the beginning of our life influence levels of neuro-transmitters in our brains. The physical structure and neural connections are altered irrevocably according to what the child experiences.

Modern developmental psychology has focused on many different influences. While some emphasize the relationship between mother and baby, others stress the importance of key events, positive or negative, in the early years and their influence on brain chemistry and emotional memory.

It is vital to remember that theories are merely maps and that they need to be checked against reality to make sure that they work. The common underlying theme in all of these maps is that certain pleasant and unpleasant events take place very early in our lives from the moment of birth – if not within the womb – and have indelible influences on our adult self. The first pleasant/unpleasant experiences will lead the child to develop its own logic which will select the choice of least harm. It will then apply this logic repeatedly according to the demands of the situations it encounters.

This repetition will lead to the development of identifiable aspects of our overall personality, which is made up of our different subpersonalities* and these will organize themselves along the lines of the choice of least harm. A certain number will be more prominent than others but all will be interconnected, and even the lesser ones will exert some influence on the others.

Each subpersonality is made up of a series of more or less important thoughts and emotions and beliefs that form a coherent structure.

The subpersonalities will determine the scenarios, the situations, the relationships which we will encounter throughout our

* The concept of the subpersonalities is a key feature of Psychosynthesis.

life. The subpersonalities form in infancy and will grow or diminish as we age. The way in which the subpersonalities interact can best be understood by using the final map.

> The way we work is mechanical. Thought runs through the same neural circuits, triggering the same emotions. These networks add up to a series of distinct aspects, our different subpersonalities.
> They propel us into the same behavior patterns, which then set off the repetitive scenarios of our lives.

THE FOURTH MAP: THE AMPHITHEATER
or how our subpersonalities interact

Let us imagine a one-thousand seat amphitheater with a center stage on which stands a microphone. Close to the stage, seats are reserved for three stars, then two rows for twenty VIPs. The other nine hundred and seventy seven places are taken up by regular spectators.

The three stars represent the three basic programs: the program whose function is to never let go of the primary identification linked with the pain of birth; the program that makes us go towards the pleasant and avoid the unpleasant; and the program of the choice of least harm.

The three stars will direct the play of our life. They will be conditioned by certain events such as the pain of birth; incidents during the first two years of development; a severe childhood trauma - the loss of a parent or some genetic predisposition. They may also be linked to a happy childhood: there are no fixed rules.

The VIPs are compensatory behaviour patterns that keep recurring. We soon realise that each member of the audience in the amphitheater is in competition with all the others to seize the microphone. This microphone represents consciousness and to have access to it is the only way that they can gain power.

The longer one member of the audience holds on to the microphone, the more energy he acquires, the more others fight to replace him so that they too can gather energy.

When someone experiences anxiety, an addictive subpersonality generated during a time of maternal deprivation grabs the microphone and lights a cigarette. Next the self-critical subpersonality bounds onto the stage. It developed through early childhood experiences of a distant and demanding father figure, and it will do everything to grab the microphone away from the addictive one. This subpersonality then recruits help from the binge eater, who grabs the microphone and raids the fridge.

The other nine hundred and seventy seven places in the amphitheater consist of our memories, in other words of all our past identifications. So, for instance, one day while driving you catch sight of a poster of a girl wearing a red dress. The next moment the memory of a girl in a red dress to whom you were attracted years back surfaces and grabs the microphone. As this memory is not that recent, it lacks energy and cannot hold onto the microphone for long. It is soon replaced by another memory, another perception, another emotion linked to the same subpersonality, or a different one, and so on.

As we observe the amphitheater, we realize that it is the site of considerable conflict for the multiple personalities in it. They ceaselessly struggle with each other to seize the microphone and to hang on to it as long as possible.

This explains why we are subject to linguistic, visual or auditory slips in attention. Reading a newspaper, we superimpose one word on another. Some time after seeing the poster with the girl in the red dress, you turn to the classified section in a newspaper. One of the ads offers a reward for finding a dog called Rex and instead you read the word sex!

The amphitheater is a battlefield where there are no rules, where alliances form so that one or another group can have its time at the microphone, and where betrayal is a constant. From this seething mass a number of dominant groups arise: our subpersonalities.

These subpersonalities are in constant flux. Their powers may vary but their core is always built in the same way. It is made up of repressed pain, which is then overcompensated. Collectively, they form your psychological identity.

Just as different governmental agencies are in competition for a share of the budget, our subpersonalities compete to have access to the conscious mind.

Once we have understood the nature of this highly competitive field within us, we will say: yes, this is how I function, with unconscious structures running my life, but what should I do about it? Having thought this through, the only thing to do is to develop the ability to observe ourself.

This first chapter provides you with two keys that will help you during the journey, along with the four maps of our conditioning. We can only advance on the path of self-knowledge – and that means on the path of our de-conditioning – if we understand the nature of the elements that condition us. We must never forget that however good a map is, it is only a representation. It invites us to travel and shows us what road to take, but it is never the road itself.

PREAMBLE TO THE PSYCHOLOGICAL WORK

By applying the techniques described in this book, you will begin a journey within yourself. You will soon achieve rapid results and in a few months your life will change. The more you work on yourself, the more you master the techniques, the more the seeker within you will grow.

As your understanding of identification and duality improves, you will be able to put the two keys to good use. The four maps will also explain how you function mechanically. Learn to use these maps. The one that shows you the link between fear and guilt; the one that shows what the choice of least harm is for you; the one that explains how the different parts of you have been built; and the one that shows you what part of you is centre stage and in control.

The fundamental element that you will be working with is fear. Your psychological structure has been built to manage it. Note that you experience two types of fear: an instinctive fear that you share with all mammals and that is felt whenever your physical security is at risk; and another fear that is illusory, that triggers anxiety and by which you are often possessed.

You will learn to observe that this fear is linked to guilt. You will acknowledge what it has created in your life. Then, using the right tools, you will be able to dismantle it and, finally, to let go of it. You should also remember that raising your level of consciousness will put your old identity at risk and that it will always resist. Whenever you keep forgetting an essential word or phrase which has struck you, you are on the right track. This blocking mechanism is clearly described in Dr Collins's foreword.

CHAPTER II

THE FIRST D: DISTANCING
or how to develop the observation of your self.

As a rule, you will start to work on yourself when hit by a crisis or a set back. If you apply a minimum of intellectual honesty to your situation, you will see that you have often damaged your life as well as the lives of those closest to you.

As long as you accept responsibility for the situation in which you find yourself and see that it is entirely down to the choices that you have made, you will come to the conclusion that different structures within you are working towards opposing ends. For when you succeed in any activity, you are more or less unified while the rest of the time you want something yet wander off in the wrong direction. So, for instance, you yearn to be in good health but eat poorly, do not exercise and drink or smoke. You want to be loved but behave badly. You want to be rich but are blocked by your unconscious losing choices. Divided, you are a field of contradictory desires.

The ability to recognise that there are within you structures that block your progress by working against each other will empower you to change your life.

You suspect that a certain logic keeps your consciousness a prisoner of its inner conflicts. It is only by developing an observer within yourself that you will be able to grasp this logic and that your level of consciousness will rise. This power of observation, this development of an observer, is called Distancing.

Distancing is a technique that will allow you to create a wit-ness* in yourself. This witness will help you to understand better what you are made of. For unless you observe your thoughts and feelings, how will you ever grasp the nature of the psychological engines that drive you?

It is important to realise that when you are not immersed in your thoughts, you are aware of them, but when you are immersed in them, you are not aware of them.

While reading a book, you may have to go back ten or fifteen lines. Your eyes scanned the text but your attention was taken from it by another train of thought. You carried on reading without being aware that you were no longer engaged by the text.

You will also notice the following phenomenon: when not immersed in your thoughts, your attention shifts instantaneously into an increased sensitivity towards your body. Take this opportunity to concentrate on your breathing. Observe how this connects you to your body and how it reduces the impact of your thoughts. As soon as you divide your attention, the frequency of your thoughts diminishes.

The way in which your system of identification functions is by setting up a series of grabbing points. It does this all the time and at every level, thereby maintaining your ego, maintaining the subject-object dynamic, maintaining duality. As a result of mental turmoil, you flit from one thought to another. You do not live in the real world but in a world made up of the projections that come from your experiences. You do not live life; you experience life through the filter of your perceptions and mental habits. So, for example, you often visit a man in an office who sits behind a desk above which there hangs a painting. One day you go to see him and the painting has vanished. You do not see the wall but the absence of the painting. Your ego has used an element of your memory to create an identification.

To understand the logic that drives your thoughts and feelings, you must create a new grabbing point whose nature will be different from your thoughts and feelings. Once you have established a distance from your mental identifications, you will be able to observe them and from there understand the mechanisms that drive them.

THE PRACTICE OF DISTANCING

The practice of Distancing hinges on the ability to divide your attention between your thoughts and feelings on the one hand, and your sensory perceptions on the other.

The key element in this practice is to see that as soon as you are no longer immersed in your thinking processes, you connect to your sensory perceptions. You will learn to use these sensory perceptions to create a witness* of yourself.

You see at first that while your attention can easily focus on one sense, it has difficulty embracing two or three sensory fields at the same time. What you have to do is to transform several sensory fields into one. Focus on one sensory field, sight, for example. Open your perception further and add hearing. You have now unified sight and hearing in one field. Open your field of perception even more and add the weight of your body. You have now unified sight, hearing and the feeling of the weight of your body into a larger field.

As you unify sight, hearing and the weight of your body in a single field of perception, you will notice that your system of identification is disturbed. You will observe your attention moving rapidly from sight to hearing, from hearing to the weight of your body, from the weight of your body to sight. You now understand that within you there is a mechanical aspect that constantly seeks grabbing points, or identifications.

You are a little like a TV that is being switched rapidly from one channel to another. You also grasp that the logic that makes you switch from one sense to another when you try to unify three senses into a single field of perception is the same as the one which made you see the absence of the painting rather than the wall behind the desk. This mechanism of identification, of grabbing points, is the very nature of your psychological entity.

After practicing this exercise for a short while, you will be able to see and to hear and to feel your body at the same time. This exercise will, of course, become a new identification, a new grabbing point. But once you have established this new grabbing point, you will no longer drown in your thoughts and feelings. If you find it difficult at the beginning of this practice to unify two or three sensory fields at the same time, remain conscious of your in- and outbreath or of the weight of your body on the chair, allowing the film of your thoughts to screen before you. The main thing is to divide your attention between one or several sensory perceptions on the one hand, and the film of your thoughts and feelings on the other.

It is important to make the moments that you are conscious of your thoughts and feelings last as long as possible. If you put a little effort into it, you will develop Distancing, the key exercise in the observation of your identifications.

The crucial point is not to become immersed in the flow of your thoughts and feelings. By concentrating your attention on unifying two or three sensory fields, you will not be carried away by your mental processes, you will not respond to the thoughts and feelings that come up within you.

Clarity, stillness and an absence of reaction will define your new stance. From this stance, you will observe the flow of greed, anger and fear just as you note kindness, generosity and affection;

that is to say you will not judge, condemn, nor approve and, above all, you will draw no conclusions.

With a little perseverance you keep this observer of yourself in a state of attentiveness while the other parts of you come and go on the screen of your mind. Even though you can feel the degree to which this observer is drawn towards mental activity, you will, by keeping your attention divided, remain conscious and above the mental flux. And when your thoughts and feelings begin to unfurl once again, you are no longer identified with them.

Thoughts and feelings flow before you but you are detached from them. By expanding the field of your perception, you have maintained the division of your attention.

Your ego has now created a new grabbing point, another identification, namely the sensory perceptions that it must endeavour to keep unified and onto which it must now focus. The frequency of your thoughts and feelings diminish. As a result, you can see their movements with greater clarity and are much more conscious of them.

> **By thinking less, you disengage from anxiety. Distancing frees you from it.**

All you have to do is to keep practicing.

Remember the amphitheater in which the subpersonalities are in constant conflict and keep vying for the microphone? Well, you must now train a part of your ego to remain in a state of vigilant silence at the top of the amphitheater and to observe the activity below.

In so doing, you are training a special form of attentiveness that no longer triggers a reaction. This attentiveness directed at your inattentiveness turns into a vehicle that lets you travel to the heart of your conditionings.

At this stage the important thing is not the length of time that you manage to maintain Distancing, but the frequency per hour, per day that you remember to engage in the process.

To start off, you will manage to watch your thoughts or feelings ten or fifteen times per day. Then, little by little, you will build up to one hundred, two hundred, three hundred times until this new behaviour pattern becomes an increasingly stable position.

You may consider that one hundred, two hundred, three hundred times per day is an incredible amount. But consider the number of thoughts and feelings you have every day – over fifty thousand!

Distancing is non-reactive attentiveness, based on physical sensations. It offers a sense of peace, an inner ease that you will never have experienced before.

As a result of this sense of peace, of this new security, you will see in yourself things that you would otherwise have repressed. You begin to perceive yourself differently, rather like the first time you examined yourself in a three-sided mirror and discovered what you looked like in profile, or heard your voice recorded, or caught sight of yourself on film.

It is not until you have seen in yourself things that you had not seen before that the work has begun.

You must now train a part of yourself to witness the way in which the other subpersonalities in the amphitheater constantly jockey for position.

This training must be applied with discipline for your subpersonalities, your various contradictions, are always vying to take over the microphone, in other words, consciousness. It is only when they have grabbed your attention that those different parts of you can gather the energy that will reinforce them. Everything seeks to grow on the physical, the psychological and the psychic level. Why is getting rid of a bad habit so hard? Because the energy that has been invested in this habit is much greater than the part of you that wants to lose it.

The practice of Distancing is to encourage an aspect of yourself never to seize the microphone. This new aspect of your ego is not a subpersonality that belongs to your old history: it is a neutral attentiveness linked to the unification of three fields of perception. Through this practice, you create a new center in a small part of the amphitheatre, a non-judgemental viewpoint which can only come from this new neutral space.

Now that you have established a witness at the top of your amphitheater, it must learn to watch the subpersonalities as they fight, forge alliances and betray each other in their bids to seize the microphone. This witness must never judge, project or come to any conclusions about them. For were it to do so, it would hold onto the microphone and, being in identification, would no longer be able to witness anything.

This absence of judgment and of projection is Distancing.

It has borne many names. The Buddha calls it 'the establishment of attention'. Jesus in the Gospel according to Thomas advises us: "Be like a passer-by". Hinduism refers to 'the position of the witness'. Shantiveda speaks of 'the guardian of the spirit' and Gurdjieff names it 'the remembrance of the self'. Until this position is securely established, it is impossible to put order in one's life.

You now understand that at its lowest level the psychological structure is made up of fear and guilt. Fear and guilt are repressed and counterbalanced by desire. As soon as a desire is satisfied, it is replaced after a short interval by another. If it is not replaced, anxiety will often come to the surface.

The nature of the mind is best defined as agitation and movement. It has built itself on the repressed emotions of the past. Thoughts and feelings constantly mix, interconnect and self-generate, making up the psychological entity. If you think of your mental and emotional life as a storm, as a mechanical whirlwind, what you need to do is to create an eye at the center of this personal storm. Every moment spent in the eye of the storm out of the reach of your automatic, habit-bound behavior makes it grow and opens up a better quality of life.

Only through the process of neutral observation can you begin to put order into your life. The key lies in watching your thoughts and feelings as an observer may watch passers-by in a street or as train passengers may gaze on an unfolding landscape.

This observation must be neutral and uninvolved like that of a wise old man observing children in a playground. There are sweet and intelligent, brutal and cruel children and he watches them all with the same benevolent detachment.

"My spirit must be under careful watch and well guarded. For apart from the exercise of watching one's self, what are all the others worth?"

Shantiveda. VIIth century.

The exercise of watching one's self, of establishing attention, of setting up the witness position has long been taught by the teachers of non-dualistic philosophy. No progress can be made on the path of self-knowledge, and thus no change in your life can occur, unless you develop an observational tool. This will permit you to bring unconscious structures into the open.

IN SUMMARY

Distancing is a powerful technique that needs to be practiced again and again. Once it has taken root, it will turn into a source of enormous satisfaction for there is no greater pleasure than the exploration of one's self.

Distancing allows you to create a witness of yourself that will help you to

• Understand the mechanism of identification.

• See the rhythm and impact of your dysfunctions.

CHAPTER III

THE SECOND D: DISCERNMENT
Or how to deepen the knowledge of yourself

Just as the first D, Distancing, has helped you to observe your self, the second D, Discernment, will teach you to dig into and dismantle your psychological layers. These two Ds work hand in hand. You will, as a result of this combined practice, develop a deeper understanding of the mechanisms that rule you. Your life will change because, no longer bound to old behavior patterns, you will be able to make new and better choices.

UNDERSTANDING THE DYNAMIC OF THE SUBPERSONALITIES

Distancing has allowed you to see the nature of the mental, emotional and even physical agitation that drives you. It has also taught you to see the way in which the subpersonalities fight to have access to the microphone.

Now that Distancing has become part of your daily practice, you understand what the subpersonalities are. They encompass a wide variety of types. Among them can be found the strong leader, the eternal optimist, the seducer, the rebellious or submissive son or daughter, the risk-taker, the do-gooder, the shameless social climber, the complainer etc.

They come and go on the conscious level, organizing your life and often causing havoc. Associating with each other in a mechanical manner, they trigger the same old behavior patterns. So, for example, Peter, a businessman, is about to close an important deal. Suddenly a greedy aspect of himself interferes and endangers the project on which another subpersonality, the planner, has been working for a long time. Next the eternal optimist will step in and pour oil on troubled waters. That achieved, the charismatic, using his magnetic power, will rush in and regain control of the situation.

You need to understand that even when one subpersonality is dominant, the others are still active, although this activity takes place outside the field of consciousness. Below the conscious level, the subpersonalities forge alliances in order to express themselves. Bonded by the logic of your habitual thought associations, they lie in wait for an opportunity to grab the microphone and control the situation. This opportunity will be set up by a powerful desire such as being in love or yearning for material success. Equally, emotions such as fear, anger or jealousy will set off a counterproductive chain reaction.

To illustrate this, take the example of Anna, a young woman whose father was a serial womaniser and whose mother was constantly depressed. One day she fell in love with a handsome and seductive man only to discover some time later that he was having an affair with her best friend. After a terrible argument with her husband about her best friend, she lost both and became depressed.

You can understand how this situation was brought about by a number of apparently positive subpersonalities: Anna's romantic subpersonality, allied to the one that wished to be confirmed by a handsome and seductive man.

Meanwhile the devalued, the victimised and the depressive parts of her lurked in the shadows, ready to exploit the next opportunity to seize control. When she discovered her misfortune, the devalued, victimised and depressive parts of her forged an alliance with an angry subpersonality. This set off the chain reaction of a violent argument that brought about the end of the marriage, followed by depression. As always, behind the victim lies concealed guilt. Had Anna been able to apply Distancing and Discernment, she need not have spent so much of her life depressed like her mother and obsessively blaming her husband. She would have seen how she had created her situation and done something about it.

THE PRACTICE OF DISCERNMENT

The second D, Discernment, consists of pushing your introspection to a deeper level in order to dismantle the causes that motivate your behavior. This practice requires the ability to identify the part of you that is in power, the one that acts at a conscious level.

You will ask yourself the questions: "Who says that? Who wants that?" By putting these again and again to yourself, you will recognize the nature of the alliances that form you: why you place yourself at great risk; why you destabilize yourself; why you keep repeating the same old behavioral patterns? How many times will you have to hit the same old brick walls before you can identify the guilt that activates your subpersonalities and that prevents your level of consciousness from rising?

Through this process, you gradually discover what has been the choice of least harm* for you. You see how this choice has driven you into a series of repetitive scenarios. You have often avoided seeing guilt by 'going towards the pleasant and avoiding the unpleasant'. This has encouraged you to tell yourself: "that will not happen to me" or "I will not do that again." A vivid example of this is the promise that the alcoholic, the drug addict, the compulsive gambler make to stop once and for all. And just like them, your basic conditioning grabs hold of you and makes you repeat what you had tried to avoid doing.

You now have a better understanding of your unconscious motivations, as opposed to those that you display consciously. For example, you consider an emotional or professional relationship important, yet systematically sabotage it. This is a clear example of the degree to which guilt possesses you. Your understanding of the mechanical structure which you are made of grows and it opens up your armour.

It is at such moments that you catch a glimpse of your vulnerable child*, which is the point of connection to your real nature. If it feels sufficiently secure to reveal itself beyond the masks that you habitually wear, it can create a very intimate rapport with another person. Love comes from letting go of the armour. For it is your vulnerability that allows you to create a loving and intimate relationship. Conversely, it is this same vulnerability that can spell the end of intimacy when, feeling at risk, it triggers your aggressive subpersonalities. Intimacy and love can only blossom if there is little or no armour. Most of the time, however, your vulnerable child* is hidden under the protective layers that it has built to defend itself.

HOW TO SEE YOURSELF AS YOU REALLY ARE

As a result of consistently practicing Distancing and Discernment, at a certain moment you see the way you behave in its full light and are profoundly shaken by the revelation. For example, you understand how you have maintained a relationship that has soured simply to avoid the emotional pain of its break-up, maintaining it being the choice of least harm. You also realize then how little you love yourself and how this losing choice represents the least harm to maintain your old structure.

> **The only way to change is to see yourself as you are and to be profoundly shaken by it.**

The effect of being profoundly shaken by what you see in yourself is that a much wider perspective of what you are is exposed, just as a zoom lens can reveal the existence of a larger field of view.

Only if you are profoundly shaken can you begin to change. For mental knots are not located in the intellectual realm but in the emotional. You will then experience sensations around the solar plexus, in the abdomen and in the shoulders. In much the way that an ice shelf fragments under the influence of the rising temperature, you will feel your old emotional structure dismantle under the force of a new energy.

WHY YOU HAVE TO SEE YOURSELF AS YOU REALLY ARE

The distinction between thought and feeling is neuro-anatomically now well understood. Buried deep in the center of the brain there is a highly specialised gland, the hypothalamus, that acts like a relay station between thoughts and feelings. Thought is the product of the neural connections in the cortex – 'grey matter' – which is developed in mammals and especially so in humans. Electro-chemical connections meet in the hypothalamus which then sends out signals to other parts of the brain and body.

The hypothalamus is linked directly to the limbic system, where emotions are experienced, and to the autonomic nervous system. When a state of fear grabs hold of you, the hypothalamus collates the information conveyed by your thoughts. It sends out the electrical and chemical messages that produce the emotions that block the throat, the stomach, and the intestines.

This helps you to understand how Distancing can intervene before the hypothalamus has produced its reflex response and has carried you along in an emotional flux. It also explains why the teachers of the different traditions have recommended the practice of Distancing. For unless this practice is firmly established, it is impossible to go beyond the barrier of the emotional lures.

To see yourself as you really are and to be shaken by it without being overwhelmed is a great step forward. For the main function of being overwhelmed by this feeling is to block the process of introspection.

The experience of being shaken will provide you with an ability to stand back and understand with greater accuracy how your ego functions. This realization will accelerate its dismantling. Remember that if you are not shaken straightaway, you will need to keep on drilling.

THE ARMOUR OF THE EGO AND ITS DEFENCE SYSTEM

Your ego is an armour, a system of defence on permanent watch. When this system is at risk, it defends itself by creating grabbing points such as lying, anger or other forms of compensation. You generate identifications to maintain your logic. When it is at risk, the ego uses lures. You now begin to understand to what extent you are subject to automatic programs and to what extent your ability to choose is limited.

Paul was abandoned by his mother when he was five. By the age of thirty-five, he has become an alcoholic. Married, he lives in fear of his wife leaving him. Every time this emotion overwhelms him, he becomes violent towards her. One day in a moment of great clarity, he sees what he has turned into and is shaken by this state of affairs. He begs his wife's forgiveness, gives up alcohol and devotes himself to helping others with drink-related issues.

A year later, Paul has become so good at solving other people's problems and is spending so much time on them that, feeling unloved, his wife leaves him. As a result, his sense of abandonment returns with such strength that he takes up drinking again.

The initial insight that made him give up alcohol put his inner logic at risk. It was built on a fear of abandonment, concealed behind alcoholism. Had Paul practised Distancing and Discernment, he would have realized that, behind his fragility, there was a fear of abandonment activated by guilt. Instead he identified with helping others beyond a reasonable level, and the praise he received reinforced this lure. Driven by his repressed guilt, the abandonment ended up causing the one thing that he had tried to avoid.

THE DIRECTIONAL EGO

The only way to avoid being caught by lures is to develop a directional ego* that practices Discernment and to create an aspect of your self that will become a seeker. This seeker is a new identification, a totally new aspect of your ego. It has sprung from the part of you that does not judge and that draws no conclusions. It has sprung from the practice of Distancing. For were it to draw conclusions, it would arise from your suffering emotional body, from your shadow*, from all the old identifications that have conditioned your life.

What defines the seeker in you is that he wants you to see what you do not want to see in yourself. The seeker will sharpen his questioning skills. The tools that he will use will be Distancing and Discernment. He will turn into your therapist and best friend.

The practice of Discernment depends on your ability to zoom back, observe, then dig into your layers.

Whenever a thought or feeling comes up, the right questions to ask are: "Who says that? Who wants that? Who feels that?" Commit yourself to this process of constant self-interrogation, and you will soon understand the nature of your subpersonalities, the different aspects of your self.

Remind yourself to ask: "Who says that? Who wants that? Who feels that?" This self-interrogation must be reinforced all the time. When you have identified your principal subpersonalities, you will complete this questioning process by asking: "Who says that? What for? To reinforce what? To protect what?"

By asking yourself: "What for? To reinforce what? To protect what?" you will flush out the layer, the subpersonality, that hides behind the one uppermost in your mind. You will start to disassemble the unconscious structures that form you, you will start to dismantle your armour. And by asking: **"Who wants that? Why? Who says that? To reinforce what? Who decides that? In what way is this choice the choice of the least harm? The choice of the least harm to reinforce or defend what aspect of me?"**, you will recognize the energy of your mother, of your father, of all the authorities that have educated, influenced and manipulated you. For these energies are locked away in the various layers of your psyche and carry the guilt of your ancestors and of those who imposed their will on you.

To illustrate this, let us look at Susan, forty-five, who is sitting at home alone watching TV when she suddenly has a craving for ice cream. As she knows how to practice Distancing, instead of raiding the fridge, she observes the craving and notices that the feeling in her stomach is the same as the one she gets when she is afraid. By asking: "Who is afraid and why", she realizes that being at home alone watching a romantic film has highlighted her lack of relationship and her loneliness. She hears her mother's voice warning her that she will never amount to much without a husband, and also remembers her mother comforting her in moments of distress by giving her food. She notices the sadness but instead of rationalizing it, she asks: "Who is sad and what for?" She sees that, beneath the fear and sadness, a part of her does not believe that she deserves happiness. Susan has made the first tentative connection with the guilt at her core which, like a nuclear reactor, provides energy for everything else.

Just as a nuclear reactor has a series of protective walls, each of her layers shielded her from experiencing the next. Had Susan not questioned herself, she might have remained stuck in her compensatory eating mechanism and not felt the fear. For fear was the choice of the least harm to protect her from sadness. Had she remained fixed in her sadness, she might have consulted a doctor and been given anti-depressants. And had she taken this option, she would have found it impossible to dig deep in herself and contact the guilt that lay behind it. When you see yourself as you really are, you are inevitably shaken by it. At that moment, the seeker that you have created in yourself will accentuate the process of zooming back and speed up the dismantling of your various layers. This will both strengthen the consciousness of the seeker and enlarge the field of your understanding.

Remember not to identify with the effects of being shaken for longer than a few seconds. For if you stay with them too long, you may lock yourself in a sadness which will maintain itself by feeding on your repressed emotional past.

Remember too that the ego will always try to hold onto its identifications for its task is to maintain duality, the subject-object dynamic, at any cost. In order to protect itself, it deploys various strategies, among which the one that operates at the conscious level is to go towards the pleasant and avoid the unpleasant.

Facing up to what is repressed is always unpleasant. That is why you must develop the quality of your observation - Distancing; and sharpen your ability to dig deep in order to see what you do not want to see - Discernment.

Whenever you are shaken by what you see in yourself, you zoom back and lose a portion of your defences. As you work on yourself, you will develop a certain sensitivity. This allows you to feel a subtle energy circulating through your body, an electrical sensation that you can feel on the surface of your face and hands. This sensation will later evolve by flowing freely throughout your body. You will then realize that mind and body are linked energetically. The mind acts on the body, the body on the mind. From this you deduce that the mind has a physical reality.

Increased awareness supports your Distancing, making it more physical, more stable and linking it to new bodily sensations. When these sensations are active, Distancing is operative. When they are no longer active, you are re-engaged in identification. Once the practice of Distancing has become more established, Discernment can go deeper and penetrate layers of which you had not previously been aware.

You have now understood that when a subpersonality arises in consciousness, it is manipulated by another part of you that lies just behind it in the unconscious. Whenever you need to make a decision, ask yourself: "In what way is this decision the choice of least harm? And least harm to reinforce what part of me?" To understand this logic, and to cut through it, is the practice of Discernment. It is by dismantling your unconscious structures that you will raise your level of consciousness and will stabilize yourself above your shadow.

"Man has within him numerous skins which cover the depths of his heart. Man knows so many things but does not know himself. Ah! Thirty or forty skins just like those of an ox or of a bear cover the soul. You should therefore excavate your foundations and learn to know yourself."

Meister Eckhart. XIII–XIVth century.

To dig into your layers means to dismantle whatever prevents your psychic embryo from growing. The development of the soul will be dealt with in the next chapter, but you should note that a great deal of the work is psychological.

It is vital that you open a space within yourself to allow the psychic being to grow. Your psychological structure will, however, resist in order to hold onto its identifications.

You are made of layers. Each layer protects the one below it, just as the first rows of the audience in the amphitheater screen off those behind. These are your defences, the protectors of your inner logic. When this logic is at risk, it resorts to lures. They manifest as powerful emotions such as anger or rage or despair, which emerge to distract your attention. They can also take the form of a mental fog that appears when certain words, certain phrases put your unconscious logic at risk and make you forget them instantaneously.

This mental fog will freeze your speed of association in order to block your introspection. When you work on your dreams, it may also act to erase them.

When faced by the seeker's probings, the ego's structure functions like a modern apartment block threatened by fire. First the sprinklers gush down from the ceiling, then the fireguards slam shut to isolate the danger.

You soon realize the extent and intensity to which these lures have possessed you and how much you still short-circuit yourself. This provides you with remarkable opportunities to understand your defence system better.

The only way to change is to see what you are and to accept it. This acceptance triggers the process of letting go. The heart of the experience of life lies in the acceptance of the now.

> "Always say 'yes' to the present moment."
>
> Eckhart Tolle. XXth century.

To practice Distancing is to accept the present. To practice Discernment is to excavate your previous layers of conditioning. By practicing these two, you can see how automatic your behavior is.

Only by discovering how mechanical and repetitive your mental processes are can you see how little you live and as a result become progressively more alive. The more you move away from your automatic reactions, the more alive you will feel. At this stage you must be careful to keep Distancing going for the cunning efforts of the audience in the amphitheater are boundless. The subpersonalities are endowed with their own mechanical intelligence, protecting themselves via a system of lures by forming alliances among themselves. An energy of fear lying below the conscious level will provoke anger. An energy of low self-esteem can give rise to jealousy. That is how your old emotional body* keeps itself going.

---

* See Glossary

KEY {

Once your consciousness is totally neutral and has become stabilized in a watchful silence, the same old lures no longer stick to the mental screen. By accepting fear, you will become free from anger. By accepting low self-esteem, you will become free from jealousy. As soon as you recognize the lower layer, the one above it is dismantled and loses its power. This is the essence of the work.

The practice of Distancing and of Discernment leads you to a better understanding of what conditions you. You recognize that these familial and collective conditionings are imprinted on every aspect of yourself from the nervous system down to the cell. They maintain themselves through grabbing points – your systems of belief – and can range from racism to respect for others, from arms-bearing to militant pacifism. Your identifications with these systems of belief constitute your different subpersonalities. The subperson-alities are made up of repetitive mechanisms that link perceptions, thoughts and emotions in a cohesive system. In the case of jealousy, for instance, a look sets off a thought association. The thought association runs through the usual neural connections before reach-ing the hypothalamus. Next an emotional response is set off, carrying you along and making you reproduce similar scenarios.

All subpersonalities trigger repetitive behavior patterns. You are as hooked on the repetition of your behavior linked to the situation that you create as the addict is to his drug. See that it is not the situation that hooks you but the emotional discharge linked to it. If you grasp this reality as it occurs and see the nature of the mechanisms that move you, a more powerful directional ego* will be born. This will help you escape from the automatic aspects that usually control you. It is then that your life will begin to change.

Once your directional ego has become firmly established above your dysfunctions, you will no longer need to reproduce your old patterns, even though for a while they will keep coming to the surface. Remember that the directional ego is made up of the under-standing of what blocks you. When you have raised your level of consciousness, you have moved from the illusion of having free will to having a certain amount of free will. You now experience the growing sense of having more control over your life.

To maintain this, watchful attentiveness must be your prior-ity. You understand that the fabric of sleep that envelops you can at last be torn. An aspect of your amphitheater has shifted. As a result, you are more conscious, more joyful, more alive.

IN SUMMARY

Distancing and Discernment show you the extent to which the armour that you have built prevents you from living and the extent to which fear and guilt limit you. As your level of consciousness develops above fear and guilt, you open yourself more and more to love. And as you will see in the next chapter, you will also create in yourself a space that will become the cradle of your soul.

- To practice Discernment is to question yourself in order to identify the different aspects of yourself.

- To practice Discernment is to dig into these aspects to discover those that lie behind.

- To practice Discernment is to explore the first causes of your behavior.

CHAPTER IV

THE THIRD D: DISIDENTIFICATION
Your psychological evolution or how to let go of your grabbing points

Disidentification is the result of a good practice of Distancing and Discernment. It comes from a thorough understanding of your mechanisms of identification. It is produced by working on yourself psychologically. Analysing your dreams is also of considerable help. A regular practice of silence, allied to time spent reading the mystics and the philosophers, will stimulate your growth. These practices taken as a whole will help you to let go of what blocks you.

THE DYNAMIC OF RAISING CONSCIOUSNESS AND THE OBSTACLES YOU WILL FACE ON THE WAY

You now see much more clearly that you identify all the time with the same subpersonalities and that they make you reproduce the same scenarios in your business, in your family and in your love life. Once you understand this, you can gradually disidentify from the subpersonalities that maintain your fear, low self-esteem and guilt and that lie at the origin of your dysfunctions. The more you do this, the more you create a new aspect in yourself, a directional ego capable of letting go of losing choices and of moving towards winning ones*.

Inner disturbances are less frequent. You make more winning choices instead of being pushed in the same old directions by your unresolved issues. You no longer hit the same brick walls because you have started to dismantle the internal mechanisms that keep recreating these situations. As a result, conflicts quieten down.

As the quality of your Distancing improves, your directional ego, when it is time to act, is increasingly free from the background noise of the old aspects of yourself. Your attitude towards the world begins to change. And it is when your attitude to the outer world changes that something significant has been achieved.

You now realize that all you need to do is to be alert and to allow the appropriate part of yourself to take charge according to whatever life brings up. Unfortunately, seeing the situation through the prisms of attraction, repulsion, fear, anxiety and escaping into compensatory behaviour, you often manipulate the situation to your own disadvantage.

You have long maintained an unconscious conflict between what you believe yourself to be and what you really are, between your surface level and what lies below. This not only blinds you but also forces you into consuming enormous amounts of energy. Most liars insist that they never lie. Most con men repeat that they are honest. Whenever you keep saying something, you can be sure that you unconsciously carry the opposite structure. And when you insist that everything will be fine, it is obvious that, buried in yourself, there is another aspect convinced of the very opposite. These repressed structures blur your vision of reality. They are grabbing points, identifications, from which you will have to disengage little by little.

Your old mechanisms of identifications, based on repressed emotions, engender a chronic anxiety. This makes you project into the future, immersing you in a world disconnected from reality.

This anxiety feeds the fear and guilt that lie at the base of your ego.

You need to see how anxiety stimulates uncertainty which, in turn, entertains the dilemma between positive and negative, for and against, the choices that you make and those that you put off until later. You understand how you feed this process, which is the choice of least harm, to maintain your ego.

You also start to understand how thought works. Experience nourishes memory. Conscious memory produces knowledge. The logic of unconscious memory will produce thoughts and emotions which will make you reproduce the same patterns of behavior. This mechanism maintains itself ceaselessly but as you become conscious of it, you disidentify from it.

There are moments when you see clearly that thought is separate from you and that you are the plaything of the projections-identifications that come from your past and that keep you stuck on your old merry-go-round. Increasingly aware that you should act in tune with the ever-changing situation, you project less and less. The reason why you are now able to say yes to situations where you were uncertain before is because your fear has diminished. The energy available to you increases and your creativity, your magnetic power, the very best parts of yourself rise to the surface and are strengthened.

Each situation begins to turn into a game and into a source of pleasure. From now on, it offers an opportunity to bring out of you the part best able to sort it out. You find yourself less and less locked in those aspects of yourself not able to cope with life. As a result everything becomes easier. From time to time fear and anxiety reappear, but they are seen for what they are, old patterns keen to keep in place what is repressed.

Remember that behind fear lies guilt. Fear is the tip of the iceberg that surges into your consciousness whereas the part that lies beneath the surface is guilt. Fear feeds guilt and has an agenda of its own. If you grasp that, you can also see that fear is man's worst enemy. It conditions your perception of the world and colors your projections. Yet in a way fear can also be useful as it shows you where you should dig deep in yourself, where you should understand yourself better and where you should love yourself.

You now understand with greater clarity how your mechanisms of fear and guilt attract what reinforces them. But be aware that this basic structure can be dangerous, sometimes even fatal.

"If you are struck down by a mortal illness, change town and change your name."

Kabbalah.

Your old identifications lie at the root of what you experience. Modify some of these and you disempower your guilt. By installing a new program, you inject a fresh dynamic into the primary causes and therefore the effects that spring from them will be different. That is why Jesus, after he had healed the sick, would say: "Sin no more" so that they would stop feeding the unconscious guilt that had created the illness in the first place.

Life is in the present, the past is gone, the future is in the process of becoming. Fear and guilt are linked to the past. Anxiety is linked to the future. Anxiety generates a future conditioned by the past. You now see that you are becoming progressively free of it. True life is in the present and is on a higher level than the mind.

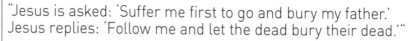

"Jesus is asked: 'Suffer me first to go and bury my father.' Jesus replies: 'Follow me and let the dead bury their dead.'"

Matthew 8.22.

Reader, are you alive? A little, truly, madly, or not at all?

Think of a place, a hotel or a house in which you had a happy or an unhappy experience. Some time later you revisit the place and note how your ego cloaks itself in the satisfied or unsatisfied feelings of the past. It projects onto everything and short-circuits the present. Once you understand the mechanisms that hold you in their grasp, you will see how little life there is in you.

The mechanism of identification searches all the time for what reinforces it. In the street a pregnant woman notices other pregnant women, a soldier spots other soldiers, the owner of one type of car recognises the same model. The nature of the ego is to look for grabbing points.

The mind is a non-entity that tries to reinforce its illusory existence on a permanent basis. It can neither see reality as it is, nor accept it. It creates identifications by using memory to maintain itself. But if you can force it to confront itself, it will suddenly disappear. You feel this sense of universality just as when you face a wondrous sunset, look into a baby's eyes, contemplate a work of art, listen to a classical concert, or when you are involved in an occupation that absorbs you fully. The energy of life then shoots right through your layers and for a few moments you feel connected to another dimension.

Disidentification is the process by which you move from a mechanical state to a dynamic state. A part of you has become more alive, even if the other parts have not yet gone through a major transformation. Disidentifying means to inject more life into your life. As you increasingly see yourself as you really are, you are sorry about what you see but do not identify with sadness. The experience can sometimes be unpleasant if, instead of surrendering your identifications, you struggle against them. You also feel the resistances that your emotional body* puts up. Those resistances are lures and their function is to distract consciousness in order to block your progress, to make you lose your Distancing.

It is important to realize that the lures will always be around as they are the defence system that protects your ego. As you raise your level of consciousness, they will be increasingly active.

At this stage, they fall into three categories.

The first category is the hardest to overcome : whenever you judge or come to a conclusion, you are identified with that judgment or that conclusion and the position of Distancing has been lost. Be aware that you do that all the time.

Secondly, whenever you identify with an irrational emotion, irrational with regard to the situation – such as an irrational desire to cry, an irrational outburst of anger, any emotion that flares up in order to block the process of introspection – Distancing and Discernment are no longer operative.

Thirdly, whenever a mental fog settles over you, it makes you forget what you have just heard, or blocks your understanding, or sends you into a sleep-like state, or erases a dream that you had partly recalled.

You understand that whenever the ego is at risk, it defends itself using lures. But it does so mechanically and therein lies its weakness. Through consistently practicing Distancing, you have created a new intelligence, an intelligence that is less reactive, less mechanical. It is this intelligence that can detect the lures. As soon as they are recognised as such, they lose their power and show you where you have to dig.

> **Three categories of lures protect the ego. Their function is to block the raising of consciousness by interrupting introspection:**
>
> **When you judge or come to a conclusion**
> **When you are seized by an irrational emotion**
> **When you are seized by mental fog**

The more you evolve, the more your ego's old logic is at risk. It will therefore try to sabotage any increase in awareness by bringing you down. Fortunately this does not last long for life soon takes you in hand as it seeks itself through you. Life seeks consciousness, evolution being proof of this. The more you raise yourself above your dysfunctions, the less likely you are to fall. You also understand that the reason you fall is to prepare for the next ascent.

The situations you experience are an opportunity to accelerate your evolution. The conflicts you experience on the outside are no more than the reflections of your inner imbalances. The world provides you with opportunities to observe, question and change yourself. In the same way your unconscious world offers you guidance through your dreams. Learn your very own symbolic language and you will understand that you have an intelligence that keeps telling you which situation you are in, what aspect of yourself you should focus on and how your shadow blocks you.

Read and re-read the chapter on dreams that you will find in the second section of this book*. Open your dream laboratory and in a short time you will be amazed to discover that everything in you is designed to help you get to the next stage of your evolution.

THE IMPORTANCE OF BALANCING YOUR MASCULINE AND FEMININE SIDES

An intimate relationship, in its emotional and sexual dimensions, always reflects your masculine and feminine sides.

This kind of relationship provides you with an opportunity to balance your masculine and feminine sides (animus/anima, yang/yin). Your masculine side is the aspect that allows you to act. It consists of the rational qualities that spring from your left brain. Your feminine side represents the creative and intuitive aspects that spring from your right brain. If you are a man, you need to develop your feminine aspects to help balance your masculinity. If you are a woman, you need to do the opposite.

Three sources of wisdom, coming from different traditions, emphasize how important it is to keep both masculine and feminine aspects in balance.

"A man should always be male and female so that his faith remains stable and the presence never leaves him."

The Zohar.

"He who recognizes himself as a male but behaves like a female is at the very center of the world. Virtue is always with him and he becomes as a little child."

Lao Tzu. 4-5th century BC

"Jesus said: 'When you make the Two into the One, the interior into the exterior, the inferior like the superior and the male into the female, then you will enter the Kingdom of God.'"

The Gospel of Thomas. 1st century.

These teachers point out how vital it is to balance your masculine and feminine energies. If the two poles are not in proper balance, a conflict will arise. This will effect both the building up of your identity and the defence of your self-image and as a result your relationships with your own and with the opposite sex. These interferences will create and recreate the same old conflicts. This will generate identifications that will maintain the ego, the personal entity, and that will block the raising of consciousness and, ultimately, awakening. An intensive practice of Distancing and Discernment will diminish the interferences and most of the conflicts.

Intimate relationships are a highly effective mirror. You are attracted to someone when that person carries aspects of some of your sub-personalities that have been buried either because they have not been accepted or because they have not had a chance to blossom in you. This is why you admire in the other person the qualities that you have not developed. The other person then becomes the means by which they can be expressed. Falling in love is often a matter of projecting unconscious subpersonalities onto another person. Once the energy of these subpersonalities has been expressed, the vulnerability that lay below them appears and stimulates unconscious bonds, such as father/son, father/daughter, mother/daughter, mother/son. Thereafter the relationship is likely to evolve into zones of conflicts that send you right back to those emotionally unresolved areas of yourself. As soon as you have understood that, you stop blaming others for characteristics that are yours.

By defusing old conflicts, you can avoid the suffering generated by the repetition of a scenario that will inevitably occur if the primary causes that brought it about are not dismantled.

Remember that the problem lies in you, not in the other person. It is you who has accepted or attracted this person into your life. Your inner logic always knows with what type of energy it connects. Unconsciously, you know more or less what will occur before it does. You see this in others when they repeat the same patterns of behavior, but see it poorly in yourself. Everyone has had a friend who fell in love with the wrong person. However much you tried to warn him, he would not listen. Time passed – six months, a year, two years – and your friend's life had become a nightmare.

The unconscious logic that pushed him into this situation knew the energy with which it was about to connect. What you can see in your friend, you must be in a position to detect in yourself at the right time. To achieve this, you need to maintain a good quality of Distancing and to have a directional ego strong enough to allow you to disengage from potentially painful situations. As your rate of progress increases, you understand much better the mirror effect of your environment.

You realize that if you keep seeing someone who is dishonest, it is because you carry these same structures buried somewhere within you.

"First take the log out of your own eye, and then you will see clearly to take out the speck that is in your brother's eye."
Matthew 7.5.

When you become conscious of what you have repressed, you abandon the negative criticism of others and replace it with positive self-criticism. Positive self-criticism is synonymous with intellectual honesty. It is not a judgment. It is an assessment that allows you to see aspects as they are within yourself without labelling them good or bad. That is the only way in which you can disidentify from them.

Through this letting go, you feel a new energy moving through your body that then becomes lighter. As you start to dismantle your psychological structure, a more subtle, tactile space opens up within you. As a result of the changes that you have made in yourself, your partner will also evolve. And your relationship will spontaneously rediscover the freshness that it had lost.

HOW TO ACHIEVE YOUR HOPES AND ASPIRATIONS

To achieve your hopes and aspirations, you need to see reality as it is, not as you project it. To succeed in life, it is necessary to define your objectives clearly.

Without a directional ego, nothing is possible. As a rule, a good education provided by well-adjusted parents will allow you to build a directional ego. If it has not been built, an intensive practice of the first two Ds, as well as working on the symbolic language of your dreams, will help you to do so.

The directional ego is that part of you which makes decisions that are in harmony with your goals and are related to the reality of the situations you encounter. If you do not have a directional ego, or only an undeveloped one, situations will be seen through the prisms of different subpersonalities that have contradictory objectives. As a result, you will superimpose on most situations anxiety, doubt or irrational optimism, none of which has anything to do with reality.

No matter your position in life, economic stability is an invaluable base if you wish to have enough time to learn about yourself. Unless that base is relatively stable, it means that your systems of guilt are active and that your logic of losing choices is still operative. If that is the case, it will be difficult to make progress for you only have a certain amount of energy available.

By this stage, you have understood and integrated a large part of your psychological mechanisms. As you have also dismantled some of your unconscious structures, they rule your life less and less. You now know that consciousness is the point from which orders are given and that the unconscious executes them to the best of its abilities according to the load of fear and guilt that it carries.

You have grasped that thought is energy and has a physical reality. If it is controlled consciously, it can be a positive creative energy.

> **Consciousness decides, the unconscious executes. All you need is to be aligned.**

So, for example, you are at A and want to go to Z. Hold Z in mind, visualize it and keep it in the present. You may have to go via C, E, Y and W. You have no way of knowing how the journey will turn out for it is in the nature of things to change constantly. Hold Z at the forefront of your mind and relax totally. Remember that fear and anxiety will often lock you in a losing strategy.

As you can do nothing unless the situation demands it, do nothing and wait for events to unfold. Remain focused. Keep Z in the present for it to materialise. To achieve your hopes and aspirations, you need to see reality as it is, not as you project it.

To keep Z in the present implies creating a part of yourself that does not doubt. Positive thinking, a key topic today, only works if you are relatively unified. If your conscious self harbours no doubt, but seventy to eighty per cent of your unconscious fear and guilt systems have not been dismantled and are still operative, it will never work. To make things manifest, the majority of you must be unified. Through digging and dismantling, you disidentify from the mass of residual guilt and fear, and that is how you harvest the fruits of Distancing and Discernment.

To be unified is to have faith and faith only becomes active once you ride your shadow. Faith is the absolute conviction of a reality of which you do not yet have concrete evidence.

"Conscious faith is freedom.
Emotional faith is slavery.
Mechanical faith is stupidity."

Gurdjieff. XXth century.

Things exist first on the virtual plane, then on the potential and, finally, they manifest.

To illustrate how the virtual manifests, take the election of President Obama. Films such as Deep Impact and TV series such as 24 made the election of a black President possible. This virtuality took further form when Barack Obama began to think seriously about becoming a candidate. It became potential the day that Senator Obama threw himself into the race for the White House. His desire, in harmony with this potential, manifested in an election that many had regarded as highly unlikely.

The knack of making things real lies in bringing them from the virtual through to the potential and on to the manifest without allowing fear and anxiety to interfere. The more you are alert, the more conscious, the more unified you are, the stronger is your ability to manifest what you want.

Through the practice of Distancing, you have developed a conscious ego, a witness. It is a part of you that does not judge, that draws no conclusions. This witness is increasingly stable and attracts in an instant, without your intervening, the subpersonality that matches your situation. As you begin to ride your shadow, your magnetic power, your capacity to convince others, becomes stronger.

You now know how to say yes and how to say no for you have identified the parts of you that had difficulty saying no. You have linked those parts to the system of fear, of low self-esteem and guilt that were always in the background. These systems are still there and will always be there, but they do not have the power to take hold of you in the same old way. You repress less and less the energies of anger, jealousy, fear, shame, and guilt. As you observe and discern them, they lose a portion of their strength. Through the practice of Discernment you have now managed to build a directional ego of increasing power that remains fixed to its objectives and that is decreasingly caught by those parts of you that are still connected to fear and guilt. Remember that the directional ego will always be reinforced by how well you understand your shadow, your dysfunctions.

As a result of having modified your inner life, your attitude towards the outer world has changed. Knowing yourself better, you become more understanding of others. Because you love yourself more, you no longer sabotage your own plans and are not attracted to negative relationships. Your mind becomes an increasingly effective tool. You solve your problems because your level of consciousness lies above the level that created them. You have moved from a logic of unconscious losing choices to a logic of conscious winning ones. You become the conscious creator of your life. You no longer project into a future determined by past emotions.

By seeing where you do not love yourself, you learn to love yourself more. Understanding dismantles the armour that prevents love from expressing itself. True love springs at the same time as understanding. To open your heart, you must have dismantled your fears. Only then will you be able to love others.

> **To leave behind unconscious losing choices and to go towards conscious winning ones, ask yourself at least twenty times per day: "This part of me that is active now, is it a winning one or is it a losing one?"**

To achieve Disidentification, you must practice Distancing regularly. You must stand back from mental activity and allow the different subpersonalities to move freely within you without interfering. When practicing Discernment, you know better to which subpersonality most thoughts, most feelings belong; and you also know whether they are linked to fear, low self-esteem or guilt or to the directional ego that rides them. The more you disidentify from what comes from the shadow, the more the seeker will acquire energy, and the less chaos you will have to deal with in your emotional and professional life. Your directional ego searches out what is good in you and gives it priority. As a result, negative thought patterns lose their power over you.

PREAMBLE TO PSYCHIC DEVELOPMENT

You are about to use a new road map: that of the development of your soul. Remember that intellectual understanding is only a departure point. The important thing is to make progress on the path of your evolution. Many people develop an intellectual understanding, but remain stuck at that stage. They use this understanding to avoid the emotional suffering that comes from introspection. Through a good practice of Distancing, you have created a space in yourself free from major suffering. Through Distancing, coupled with Discernment, you make this space larger and larger and that is the field in which your soul will grow.

If you add to that a daily practice of silence lasting at least thirty minutes, you will after a few months' experience physical sensations that will bear witness to the growth of your psychic body – your soul – within your physical being. All the information you need is contained within this book. Read and reread it and, above all, search, practice and experiment.

THE THIRD D: DISIDENTIFICATION
Your psychic evolution or how to develop your soul.

You are no longer a caterpillar but have not yet become a butterfly. While the chrysalis stage can at times be uncomfortable, it is essential.

You are now aware that the limits you meet in the world are those that you have created through your own mental habits and systems of belief. Your memory constantly feeds them through repetitive patterns of behaviour.

"In order to undertake this journey, you must from the start renounce everything which may seem like a blessing but which is in fact a habit."

Gurdjieff.

The process of Disidentification is a gradual letting go of your habits. You have seen your environment change because you yourself have changed. Your life now opens up to new possibilities. You have verified that it is your inner world that conditions the exterior. It is this inner world that you must now understand, enlarge and deepen for it will be the cradle of your soul.

You have to grasp better the mechanisms of identification that maintain your ego. Vision identifies with the object seen. Hearing with the object heard. Touch with the object felt. Taste with the object tasted. Smell with the object smelled. The mind with the object thought. Through the use of the senses, of thought and of emotion, the fear-based ego, identified with the body and the mind, has taken the place of your true nature and has blocked the development of the soul. This mechanism of identification is your psychological identity. It is composed of many subpersonalities which are self-serving and which all say "I". There is a short interval between the departure of one subpersonality and the arrival of the next. As a rule, identification links you to time and this interval between two thoughts, between two identifications, is not noticed by consciousness. There is the illusion of a continuous "I". The subpersonalities support themselves through this illusion in order to be taken for the totality of yourself. The parts masquerade as the whole.

Through an increasingly constant practice of Distancing and Discernment, you will gradually disidentify from this illusion of a continuous "I" that links you to time.

"People like us who believe in physics know that the distinction between past, present and future is no more than a limited and opinionated illusion."

Albert Einstein. XXth century.

"The past and the future only exist through you.
They are one and the same.
Only you think that they are two."

Jalal ad-Din Muhammad Rumi. XIIIth century.

"You alone make time. Your senses are its measure. Let anxiety cease and time will disappear."

Angelus Silesius. XVIIth century.

Through Distancing, coupled with Discernment, the ability to dig into yourself improves and the process of letting go of old behavior patterns becomes more frequent. A sensation of presence develops free from thought, free from anxiety, free from memory. By dismantling your old emotional body, you have opened a new space in which a psychic being, a soul not linked to psychological time, begins to crystallize and grow.

You see that because you are consistently trying to live above your mental activities, another quality of life is being born within you. You have opened new spaces in yourself. You can feel this as an electrical tingling on your skin, as well as other sensations between the eyes, on the top and at the back of the head.

Within these spaces, you crystallize a new energy that makes you feel more alive and increases your range of opportunities. As it develops, this psychic body will grant you access to another quality of life, to other dimensions that are linked neither to thought nor to memory.

During the process of letting go of old behavior patterns, you have experienced how the mind and the body are energetically linked. You now feel consciousness as energy.

Modern physics has demonstrated that matter is energy.

"Matter and energy are identical."

Albert Einstein.

Today the gods, the invisible powers, the myths of your ancestors seem to correspond to an infinity of fields: quantum, magnetic, electro-magnetic, electrochemical.

You can conceive of miracles, of unexplained physical phenomena, as belonging to a natural order within which consciousness, matter and energy mix. Consciousness is energy. Matter is energy.

The right attitude to life is to be like a scientist in a laboratory. You have a physical and mental laboratory so why not experiment and create a psychic laboratory by practicing silence on a regular basis? In order to access the higher level of your evolution, you can only advance according to the light of your own experience.

You understand better and better that thought is memory. You also sense that memory short-circuits you from life.

In the knowledge that life is in the now, you begin to let go of thought and to integrate Lao Tzu's injunction:

"It is through non-action that everything is achieved."

Lao Tzu.

The secret of life is to make action spring from non-action. This is the attitude that allows you to escape from an apparently impossible situation. A good practice of Distancing is also non-action and will help crystallize a new energy in the spaces you have cleared in yourself.

Through developing your conscious ego*, your witness* and through your regular practice of silence, a part of your amphitheater is in a transformational process. A number of your subpersonalities have become more fluid, more transparent, more subtle. Molecule by molecule, thread by thread, they have connected to another frequency of being. Some have lost their relative identity, have become pure energy and have unified naturally. They are the result of a true will, of a real conscious effort. Through Distancing, the seeker in you has created a conscious ego and from there is building a soul, a psychic being.

"Happy he who has a soul.
Happy he who does not have one.
Misery and torment to he who only has the germ of one."

Gurdjieff.

In the Gospel according to Thomas, Jesus teaches us something similar.

"To he who has, much will be given. To he who has not, the little that he has will be taken away."

In Matthew 25 vs.14–30 the parable of the talents expresses the same idea.

"A rich man called his three servants and gave each talents. Two of them made the talents grow, the third returned the talent that he had been given.
        The rich man said: "Take the talent from him and give it to the one who has the ten talents. For everyone who has will be given more and he will have an abundance. Whoever does not have, even what he has will be taken from him. And throw that worthless servant outside into the darkness, where there will be weeping and gnashing of teeth."

A conclusion that is repeated in the parable of the ten pieces of money in Luke 19. vs. 11–27.

Similarly the Prophet Mohammed says:

"Amongst you there are some who will rejoin Allah while others will be sent back to the vilest ages to the extent that having had knowledge you will be deprived of all knowledge."

Koran. XXII v. 5. VIIth century.

And:

"The soul is one of the works of Allah but they have only received from its science a limited amount."

Koran. Hadith.

These teachers are very clear. The soul, the psychic being, is not in us. What is in us is the seed, the potential for the making of a soul. 10,000 salmon roe at the head of a river will, three years later, become three or four salmon. For every thousand acorns which fall from an oak tree, only one will take root and germinate. Out of ten million locusts subjected to insecticide spray, twenty or thirty of their offspring will be less prone to the toxic chemical.

Everything is linked to evolution. Today there are seven billion human beings on the planet. A certain number will become psychically alive, a certain number will awaken. Man does not escape this general rule. He either reaches the next level of his evolution or the various scattered fragments of which he is made will dissolve in the collective unconscious.

The psychic body, the soul, develops from a matrix that is formed from the physical body and the conscious ego. The conscious ego, the direct result of Distancing, is what permits every part of you to be expressed freely. Remember that when you identify with your thoughts and emotions, you are not connected to life. You are locked in a closed circuit inside yourself, inside your memory. Your psychological entity constantly provides grabbing points by going over old issues or by running away from them into addictive behaviour such as alcohol, recreational drugs, sex, work and thrill-seeking.

"The superior soul loves life, the inferior soul seeks death."
Lu Tzu. The Secret of the Golden Flower. VIIIth century.

The right attitude is to keep connecting to physical sensations in order to see the flux of your thoughts and feelings.

The practice of Distancing has enlarged the scope of your grabbing points. You are now aware that they are both sensory and mental. As soon as the flow of thoughts slows down, you open yourself up to a superior dimension and tactile sensations unfold. You can feel in your body new physical sensations for, little by little, your psychic body is being built from your conscious ego, just as in the child of twelve the first aspects of adolescence burst forth. Soon you will be able to perceive through your body the space between two thoughts for the perception of your body will have changed.

All you need to do to help the growth of this psychic being is to judge less, to draw fewer conclusions and to savor the harmony that accompanies a much calmer mind. That is achieved by stabilizing a good quality of Distancing and by practicing silence for at least half an hour per day.

THE PRACTICE OF SILENCE

To sit in silence is an essential part of the practice. It is here that your repressed structures are transformed into an energy of consciousness and light. The important thing is to be disciplined. To practice half an hour per day is the minimum. Note how much time you dedicate to your various activities. If you cannot find sufficient willpower to invest a tiny proportion of your time in your evolution, it cannot work. As usual, the important thing is to be practical. You are the scientist of your superior states of consciousness working inside your psychic laboratory. What you are doing is building a body of consciousness and light on the scattered fragments of your shadow. The basic method is to maintain yourself above your thoughts by improving your Distancing.

The various techniques of meditation have had no other goal than to stop the mind by fixing it, for example, on breathing or on an image. Do not let yourself be distracted by the lures which are going to try to interrupt your practice. Never forget that the raising of your consciousness puts your old structure at risk. You will be beset by irrational thoughts and desires linked to sex, or food, or whatever. Remember to keep an eye on the lures. Ask yourself where they come from. You will see that they are merely mechanical and that they have no intelligence at all. They spring from the shadow. It does not matter whether you are sitting or lying down as long as your level of awareness is high. With a bit of practice, you will also see that whether your eyes are open or closed makes no difference. Above all, when you begin to have psychic experiences, forget them quickly or you will use them as grabbing points that will slow down your growth.

One day you will have a psychic experience. This new consciousness will be born in you. It will arrive at the right time and when you least expect it. The bedrock of this experience will be the realization that you are not your thoughts.

The development of the soul, of the psychic being, is a progressive path. The more you raise your level of consciousness, the greater the growth of your psychic being.

Imagine a salt swamp in which sea water gradually evaporates, allowing the salt to crystallize. When the sun shines, evaporation begins and soon speeds up and when night falls, the process slows down and stops. In much the same way, the process of the crystallisation of the soul begins when your consciousness stays above your thoughts, feelings and memories. Similarly, when you are identified with your night, in other words with the thoughts, feelings and images arising from your shadow, you are controlled by mechanical functions that reproduce the same old patterns of behavior. At that moment the growth of the soul ceases.

Place yourself above your thoughts, feelings and memory, and evolution will express itself through you. The more conscious you are of this, the more it will accelerate and the more alive you will be.

To summarise, the crystallization of the soul is progressive. Through the practice of Distancing, your conscious ego becomes stronger. Discernment destructures the old psychological strata of your emotional body. Within the space that you have cleared in the emotional body, you let go of psychological time. The result is that you channel and crystallize a new energy. It is by dismantling the dense structure of your shadow and by transmuting it into an energy of light that you develop your soul.

"The method that the Ancients used to get out of this world consisted in dissolving the dregs of darkness to restore pure light."

Lu Tzu. The Secret of the Golden Flower.

You have moved above your shadow. Your level of consciousness has raised and a certain mental silence has become established. Similarly in Hindu symbology, the Gods are above their vehicles. Ganesh, the elephant God, rides his rat, Shiva his bull. And according to Taoist symbology, you are riding your tiger. A new consciousness has evolved.

You are alive on another level. Now that you have developed a psychic being, your fear of death has diminished. You know that you are sailing on the Titanic, you know what is going to happen, but you know that you have a place in a life-boat. The effect is that you are much less afraid of death.

As soon as you have distanced from fear, your consciousness rises, your ego mutates. It becomes more subtle, opening onto new fields of experience. You have now understood that thoughts have an energetic frequency and that the soul vibrates at a higher energetic frequency. The more you climb, the more likely you are to be helped for life seeks consciousness.

The building of a psychic being, of a soul, is only the next step in your growth. The goal is awakening which is as sudden as the moment of birth and death. It is the ultimate accelerator of your evolution. That is why you must pursue Discernment and keep asking: "Who says that? Why? Who wants that? Why?" while intensifying your metaphysical practice by reading the texts of the classical teachers.

IN SUMMARY

Disidentification is the next level in your evolution. It is at this stage that you create a strong directional ego that escapes from the destructive choices linked to repressed fear and guilt. Your choices are better, your life is much improved. It is at this stage that you experience breaches in psychological time. The life of the soul, the life of the psychic being, then pursues its growth. Aware that you live on another plane than the physical, your fears diminish.

Disidentification allows you to:

- Develop a powerful directional ego.

- Build a psychic body, a soul.

PREAMBLE TO THE METAPHYSICAL APPROACH

You have now reached the metaphysical part of this teaching. The goal is to gain access to where there is no access. In order to open the door that cannot open for you – for from the side on which you find yourself, there is no handle – you will need to sharpen the sword of your intelligence on the whetstone of metaphysical inquiry. The psychological work, which implies seeing in yourself what you do not want to see, will have to be pursued at the same time. It is the combination of both at the moment that you least expect it that will reveal your true nature.

CHAPTER V

THE FOURTH D: DISCRIMINATION
Or how to get rid of your final identifications

Now that the practice of Distancing and of Discernment has become firmly established, you identify less with the primary causes of your external conflicts and most of them have diminished. Life becomes more joyful simply because you are in closer harmony with it. You now arrive at Discrimination, the fourth D, which is the gate to freedom.

Whether awake or in the dream state, all you know is duality, which means the Two. You live in a permanent state of division. You are always locked in a subject-object dynamic upheld by identification. Your 'I' identifies with its object. It identifies with vision, hearing, thought and feeling. It is this 'I' that needs to be at the center of your self-examination.

The philosophers, the sages and the saints have all spoken of the One – Truth, reality, the Absolute, divine consciousness, God – as the ultimate unity.

The One is the ultimate level of consciousness. Thoughts, concepts, everything that is perceived belongs to the Two level. Your basic problem is how to change dimensions, how to make a quantum leap, how to move from the Two to the One.

Indian philosophy has elaborated two key concepts: Discrimination, which is at the heart of metaphysical inquiry, and the Leela.

The Leela is a game of cosmic hide and seek.

The One, the Absolute, divine consciousness, God, cannot know itself. For knowledge to occur, there has to be a subject and an object. There has to be a knower and a known: there has to be Two. At the beginning, when space and time arise, at the point where the universe is born, the One fragments, becomes Two, becomes multiple. From then on, the Two pursues its path to rediscover unity. Life seeks consciousness. This consciousness becomes light, galaxy, sun, planet, mineral, vegetable, animal, human. It is this evolutionary dynamic that Hinduism calls the Leela.

Humanity opens itself to intelligence. Intelligence opens itself to the ability to question yourself deeply. The ability to question yourself deeply leads to metaphysical inquiry, to Discrimination.

While you cannot grasp what you are – divine consciousness, unity, the Absolute – you can grasp what you are not – your thoughts, your emotions, your sensory perceptions. All the identifications that imprint themselves on the screen of consciousness maintain the mechanism of duality, your apparent identity.

The practice consists of constantly applying Distancing and Discernment:"Who thinks that? Who says that? Who wants that? Who feels that?"You now put these questions to yourself in a much more unified state. The energy of the questions becomes sharper and, as a result, they shake you more profoundly. Next a critical question will arise and, at that moment, you will be discriminating. "Who perceives that? What is this entity that perceives? Who is that 'I'?" When everything that you are not has been dismantled, what remains is what you truly are: the Absolute.

At this stage of the work you will find yourself discriminating between what you are and what you are not. If you have become unified through the process of Discernment and of metaphysical inquiry, through the right question your consciousness will not be able to identify any longer with any of its fragments. It will not be able to hang on to any identifications, any grabbing points. Then your subject-object mechanic collapses. As a result consciousness moves up a level. God, the Absolute, reality, the One – call it what you will – is born within you.

In the instant when your brain is emptied of its old psychological entity because it has failed to find any grabbing points, to open any neural connections, you die to your old self and are reborn to life. You no longer live life; it is life that lives through you. At that moment everything, but absolutely everything, is different. You become one with life. Fear and anxiety are well and truly dead. You are the ultimate observer.

"First form is perceived and the eye perceives. The eye is now in its turn perceived. The mind is now the perceiving subject. The mind and its modifications move at long last into the category of perceived objects. It is the spectator who in the last analysis truly perceives, and that spectator cannot be perceived."

Shankara. XIth century.

You have now understood that the ego, the psychological entity in its superficial levels, seeks what is pleasant and flees from what is unpleasant. What motivates it at its deepest levels is to maintain itself through its grabbing points. To that end, it will create identifications such as conflict, depression, torment, illness as these will do just as well as the kind of excitement that comes about as a result of a new, stimulating and enriching experience.

At the center of the psychological entity is a seething mass of old pains. This center has a mechanical intelligence that is on a ceaseless search for security. To keep creating identifications is vital to its survival. In order to exist, it superimposes itself on present events, sometimes regarding them as tedious or boring, even though they are anything but.

The ego is nothing more than a permanent will to maintain itself in duality. In its heart of hearts, it knows that it is not; in its heart of hearts, it knows that it can be destroyed. Above all, it aims not be recognized as different from what you really are. To that end it constantly seeks to distract your vigilance and almost always manages to do so by using thoughts and feelings. You should therefore gather it up with determination just as a sheep dog corrals sheep. Put it on the spot. Challenge its nature from the inside with an increasingly acute intellect. Force it to confront itself where it is not.

So, what is this ego? What is this 'I'? What is its nature? On what does it base itself? How does it maintain itself?

You feel an acute intelligence waking within you. This intelligence is linked to an electrical sensation in the body.

Again and again you ask yourself the same questions. And the more they slice into your various layers, the more their intensity gives off a scent of novelty, the more you feel pierced through and through by this interrogation.

These questions circulate around 'I' and its grabbing points.

> "You have long been trapped in the snare of identification with the body. With the sword of the knowledge that 'I am intelligence', cut this illusion and be happy."
>
> Ashtavakra Gita.

The mind has no direct knowledge of life for direct knowledge of life is external to it. The 'I' can only comprehend life through concepts and through the forms that the senses perceive. To work on yourself always puts the 'I' at risk. As this work progresses, the crudest subpersonalities in your amphitheater, whose emotional contents have not been dismantled, burst with violence into the present. You see that they superimpose themselves on the situation and that the present is therefore never truly lived. This sends you right back to the questions: "What is the 'I'? What does it experience or fail to experience? What does it perceive or fail to perceive?"

You now sense that over half of the amphitheater's audience has shifted. The inner questioning can sometimes be so powerful that it can make your very structure shake. You sense that the radical shift of a large number of your key subpersonalities may reach critical mass and set off a life-changing chain reaction. You feel your amphitheatre crumbling at its very base.

Little by little you leave behind the belief that thought equals consciousness: I think, therefore I am. You encounter moments when you integrate with sudden clarity a precise understanding of your mechanisms.

You conclude that your life experience has fed your conscious memory, producing knowledge. Fears have also fed your shadow, your unconscious memory, producing repetitive compensatory behaviour. It is the alliance of the two that stimulates thought and that in turn triggers the same kind of experiences.

You understand that everything that you think, say or do feeds the mechanism of thought that supports the idea of yourself. What is this self? Is there ultimately such a thing as yourself? It is at this point that you are really and truly Discriminating.

"What, then, is this 'I'? And what does it want?"

The body wants to go on and on. The ego does not want to let go of its identifications. The soul wants to evolve. Your true nature does not want anything. It simply is.

IN SUMMARY

Discrimination is a blade so sharp that it cuts through the last knots of your conditioning. It is only at that point that life reveals itself to itself.

CHAPTER VI

AWAKENING
Or how to get out of this world alive

Nothing leads to awakening except the dissolution of the ego.

> "You do not possess an ego. You are possessed by the idea that there is one."
>
> Wei Wu Wei. XXth century.

If you have practiced the first two Ds sufficiently, the shell of your ego cracks and fragments. The third D has opened a space in which you can grow. Now Discrimination can find a breaking point in you.

It is important to understand that awakening is a physical process. Your thoughts impregnate your neural net. Awakening consists of suddenly emptying this neural net of images, opinions, concepts, reasonings – the sum of all your identifications that make up your psychological entity.

One day a psychological crisis will pull together all the parts of yourself. Remember that it is only if you are wholly unified that awakening can happen. This crisis will propel you towards a key question such as: "What is the origin of the universe? What is the nature of reality? Who am I?" Awakening is a neural short-circuit set off by the right question. It is not the answer but the question that is essential.

The energy generated by a question that cannot find an answer rebounds on the questioner and dissolves him. Awakening occurs when the mechanism of identification fails to find a grabbing point. For when the suject can no longer lean on an object, it disappears. Awakening is the result of the ego sabotaging itself when challenged by deep metaphysical questioning.

At a certain moment, a moment of grace, a small or large crisis will make an aspect of yourself appear that you had never met before. Faced by that aspect, you will ask yourself:

"Who am I? Who is this I?"

You will then be Discriminating.

If you intensify your inquiry, you will see that 'I' is nothing more than a thought. Considering this further, you will grasp that thought comes from memory. So where does memory come from? From identification with experience, of course: I have lived through this, I have learnt that. Where does experience come from? From identification with perceptions. If I have lived this or that, it is because I have perceived this or that. The key question now centers on perception. Who perceives? You suddenly understand that everything that you know, everything that you will ever know, belongs to what is perceived, to the nature of the perceived. The ultimate question then springs up: "Can what is perceived perceive?" You suddenly see that, just as a thought cannot think, a perception cannot perceive.

"All perception implies duality but if nothing is perceived, you attain reality in non-duality".

Vimalakirti. V–VIth century.

You grasp that, by superimposing itself on original perception, the mechanism of identification separates you entirely from the present, from original perception.

The sword of Discrimination has just cut off the multiple heads of the mythological Hydra. The sum of all your identifications has collapsed. You find yourself without any grabbing points. None! Only void! You know that there is nobody, and never was anybody, to perceive anything at all.

At the very moment that you lose your grip, you integrate your real nature for you have passed through the absence of your self, the void of the Buddhists, the death of the old man of the Christians, the ceasing of existence of the Sufis. As a result, you are free. You have got out of the illusion. You have transcended this world.

Then, everything, but absolutely everything, is different. It is no longer you who lives your life but life that lives through you, and that recognizes itself as such. In that instant you have cleared your brain of the psychological entity that possesses it. Your amphitheater is empty.

You yourself – your mental reflex action, your subject-object consciousness – have disappeared. You are now out of duality. You are one with all things. You have blossomed into the consciousness of life.

It is the ability to integrate non-being that allows you to be.

In the instant you recognize that state as the state in which you have always been, you step out of time and integrate a new dimension.

Fear is dead. Anxiety is dead. You use memory but memory can no longer use you. You only think when you need to think.

Life becomes intensely joyful, sensual and blissful. You will never again be able to say:

"I think, therefore I am."

For you have moved to:

"I am because I perceive."

By pushing your questioning further, you can now see that:

"I do not perceive, therefore I am not."

and, by not being, you are free.

You have succeeded in the rare exploit of being free while being alive. You awaken to the joyful state of being without an object.

Subject and object have disappeared. There is no longer a perceived object nor a perceiving subject. They have disappeared into perception itself and this perception is infinitely full and dynamic. You are the perception of the Absolute tasting itself.

Just as Hinduism speaks of those who are born twice, you too are reborn. You have recovered the child's spontaneity and it will never be vulnerable again.

Unless you become like little children, you shall not enter into the Kingdom of God."

Jesus Christ. Matthew 18:1–4

This child knows that nothing can ever happen to him any more. He knows that he is consciousness of life itself. He knows that he is One.

"I and My Father are One."

Jesus Christ. John. 10.30.

Only this consciousness can love for its very nature is love. This is your most intimate nature and is well within your reach. All you need to integrate it is to practice.

Awakening is the sudden loss of your conditioning. It is a state free from fear. You are the whole rediscovering itself. If you recognize yourself as the essence of all things, what could you possibly be afraid of? You are life tasting itself in the joy of being.

At the moment that you understand that there never was 'you' that entered this world, you get out of it alive.

CHAPTER VII

AWAKENING: A FINAL WARNING
Or how to confront the ultimate lures

If, while seized by the question that will cut right through your ego or the illusion that is you, you see an Archangel or the Devil or God in whatever guise, remember what the Ch'an master, Lin-Chi, said:

"If you meet the Buddha, kill him!"

In other words, the ego, when it is about to totally surrender, will attempt to hang on to itself and create a final identification. It desperately needs a grabbing point to remain fixed in the subject-object dynamic. A luminous form, be it devilish or divine, possibly the Buddha, will surge up before you. This is the last trap, the last illusion, and it is where Lin-Chi's key phrase comes in. Remember how the Devil tempted Christ during the forty days in the desert and how Mara and his army of demons appeared in front of the Buddha just before his awakening. It is always the same mechanism, always the same story.

To awaken is to compel an illusion to see that it is an illusion. From the illusion's point of view, it will do everything it can to avoid this. The mind may even create mystical experiences, be they diabolical or divine according to its system of belief, in order to stay in duality. Numerous mystics from different traditions have experienced these ultimate lures. What will permit you to go beyond them is entirely linked to the quality of your Distancing.

CHAPTER VIII

TIME TO PUSH THE DOOR OPEN

"The man without any business is the one who has allowed his surface and his depth to fuse until his emotions exhaust themselves in a total absence of grabbing points."

Huang Po. IXth century.

Awakening, the encounter with God, is nothing more than the act of fusing the conscious and the unconscious to the point where there is a total letting go.

"Form is but emptiness, emptiness but form."

Buddha. The Heart Sutra. VIth century BC

The antechamber to awakening is the void.

"There is no reality to be found and that is called supreme awakening."

Buddha. The Diamond Sutra.

Every practice, every idea of reality, will create a grabbing point, an identification, which will block awakening. And yet without a practice it is impossible to progress.

* * *

To end matters once and for all, let us take Huang Po's phrase, massage it, mash it around, and pierce it through and through. Turn it into a stick of dynamite and light the fuse.

"Allow me to remind you that what is perceived cannot perceive."

By the way, do you know anything other than what has been perceived?

* * *

If that has still not done the trick, meditate on this final injunction:

| "Do not respond to what is perceived." |

Think: do you ever do anything but respond to what is perceived?

PREAMBLE TO PART II

From what you have read so far, you have seen that your ego will generate to the very end distractions, lures and decoys to maintain its position, its logic of identification. As you make your way through the Questions and Answers that follow, your understanding of the teaching will grow.

The work that this book encourages you to do is first psychological and is closely linked to your mastery of Distancing and Discernment. You will find a section in which the technique that you need to interpret your dreams is described in detail. It also takes place on the psychic level which will be addressed in the section on the Soul. Finally, the work focuses on the metaphysical, the point where you put fundamental questions to yourself. To raise your consciousness means establishing a new understanding which will need to be abandoned for the next level to be reached, just as a mountain climber, attacking a cliff face, must let go of his hold to continue his ascent.

The philosophy of the Four Ds is both a progressive and an abrupt path. It is progressive because as you raise your level of consciousness above your shadow, you transmute this repressed structure into another energy, your soul. It is also abrupt because once you have attained the summit, you will have to dive into the void. The void is the antechamber to awakening but it is only void from the point of view of the ego. From the point of view of the awakened being, everything is resplendent with the energy of the universe.

PART II
QUESTIONS AND ANSWERS

QUESTIONS AND ANSWERS
A psychological approach

Question: How can I work on myself when I am absorbed in my day-to-day activities?

Answer: You need to develop further four qualities: awareness, discipline, courage and intellectual honesty.

Anyone can have a good quality of awareness. All you have to do is to drink in moderation and not to eat too much. Get into the habit of leaving the dining table feeling still a little bit hungry. The results will be that you will live longer, be in better health and remain alert. You must, of course, steer clear of drugs. Keep to these guidelines and you will always have a fine level of awareness.

You also need a real will to change as only this will give you discipline, because without a minimum of discipline, you will not make progress. Next, you need courage to see in yourself what you do not want to see. Only if you achieve this will you dismantle the old logic that is at the origin of your present life. Remember that awakening is to bring the ego to see that it is not.

The fourth quality is intellectual honesty. Unless you are intellectually honest, you will refuse to see the dysfunctions that come from your fears, from your shadow. By working on yourself, your dysfunctions will diminish. Your seeker will grow and gain confidence by the light of the experience it has gathered and your day-to-day life will therefore be happier and more successful.

Question: So, what should I do?

Answer: Remember to practice Distancing and Discernment as often as possible while living your life to the full. Write down your dreams and interpret them by learning your own symbolic language. Practice meditation for about thirty minutes each day on an empty stomach, that is to say three or four hours after your last meal. If that is not possible, do it every other day. Above all, stick to what you have decided to do. Read metaphysical texts for at least an hour per week in two thirty minute sessions as they will stimulate your inquiry. Just as you spend time at the gym to maintain physical fitness, so you should invest time to open up new neural connections. That is the minimum necessary to put some life into your life. It is not that difficult and it will give you enormous pleasure.

Question: So I need willpower?

Answer: You need willpower and common sense. To grasp who you really are, all you have are your thoughts, feelings, physical sensations and dreams. To make psychological progress, you must build a witness and the way to do that is to use your sensory perceptions to divide your attention. You must also constantly question the logic that lies behind your thoughts and emotions in order to dismantle it. In so doing, you will make different choices and therefore change your life. By intensifying your practice, you will create a space at the heart of your shadow, at the heart of what has been repressed. Your ticket to get out of this world alive is to transform your shadow into light. If that is what you really want, you are going to have to be methodical and disciplined.

Imagine you are a test pilot in the cockpit. What do pilots do? They spend a great deal of time compiling checklists to ensure that they have not forgotten anything. To navigate towards your highest levels of consciousness, you need to set up your own checklists. Is Distancing on? Yes, I can feel the various physical signs, tingling sensations etc. Is my Discernment operative? Yes, I am questioning what part of me thinks this, what part of me feels that, what logic is driving me. Am I sharpening my questioning by reading metaphysical texts? What about my dream life? Am I recalling my dreams and interpreting them correctly? Do I practise silence for at least 30 mins per day on an empty stomach?

You also need to be aware that even as a part of you is aiming for the heights, another is setting you up for a downward spiral that may cause you to crash.

Question: How should I meditate?

Answer: Sit in silence on an empty stomach to keep a clear head. Empty your mind of thoughts as much as possible; but when they grab hold of you, let them go and focus on the meaning of the only thing of which you are certain: "I am". When you have done so, re-engage with the thoughtless state.

Question: What is the difference between meditation and Distancing?

Answer: Meditation is a general term for practices whose goal is mental silence. Distancing is a technique that allows you to observe mental processes in any situation. Mental processes maintain themselves by renewing their grabbing points in an endless dynamic. The practice of Distancing consists of dividing your attention, thereby giving to the body-mind structure, or the ego, a sensory grabbing point rather than thoughts and feelings. From this new grabbing point you can see clearly the functioning of mental processes. For it is not until you see them functioning that you can become acquainted with them.

Question: Would you discuss this technique?

Answer: Take several sensory fields – sight, hearing, touch – and unify them. During this unifying process you will find that you move rapidly from one field of perception to another, from sight to hearing, back to sight and to hearing and so on, very much like switching from one channel to another very fast on your TV. This switching effect eventually ceases and the three fields stabilize into one. If you consider the nature of this switching effect, you will understand that it is simply your ego automatically attempting to maintain its identification. Once you have unified two or three fields into one, you can see the mental processes but are no longer so powerfully identified with them because you have created another grabbing point by unifying these sensory perceptions. With your thinking processes unfolding before you, you are in a position to witness them as you have provided your ego with an activity by giving it a new identification. The result is that the rhythm of your thoughts slows down.

Question: I see what you are getting at, but when I try to do it, my thoughts seem unclear and fuzzy.

Answer: It is all a matter of practice. You have to understand what your ego is and how mental processes operate. The ego maintains itself via a support system, what I call its grabbing points. Fear and desire, the absence of clarity are all grabbing points which belong to the personal structure. The key thing is to remain conscious while dividing your attention – that is the practice. It will bring you to the point where you will see the non-living aspect of the mental processes. At the start, just be conscious of your in- and out-breath while your thoughts and feelings unfurl before you.

Question: How would you define Distancing?

Answer: Pay close attention to yourself. How many times has your mind wandered while I have been talking? How much have you been concentrating on what has been said? Distancing is to watch your inner processes as well as what is going on around you. It allows you to remain conscious of your thoughts and feelings and to see them screened before you without interfering. It also allows you to see different situations with a sharpness of vision never before experienced. If you do not develop this quality, what chance do you have of ever becoming acquainted with yourself?

Question: What about Discernment?

Answer: Without Distancing, no Discernment. The two work together. Unless you can see the thinking processes at a distance, it is impossible to understand them. Discernment shows you why you make slips of the tongue. Why, when reading a paper, you superimpose one word on another. How your different subpersonalities, or different conflicting aspects, jostle each other to have access to consciousness, creating chaos. "I want to be rich, yet keep making lousy decisions." "I love this man, this woman, but ruin the relationship." The practice of Discernment involves digging in yourself and asking as often as possible: "Who says that? Why? Who wants that? Why?" If you get into this practice, you will see that behind shyness, behind the fear of failure, behind lies, you will always find low self-esteem, then guilt. Thereafter you will see that it thrusts you into the very situations that you apparently wished to avoid.

Question: Intellectually, I got the gist of this a while back, yet not that much has changed in me.

Answer: Mental knots lie in the emotional body, not in the intellect. You have overdeveloped your intellect in order not to face up to your emotional suffering. To see yourself as you really are implies suffering, but this does not need to last longer than a few seconds. And if it does last longer, it is because you have transformed it into another grabbing point. If it links up with other repressed emotional contents, it can keep you lying on a therapist's couch going over old traumas again and again.

Question: I have been in therapy for some time now. What do you think of it?

Answer: It is a positive practice because you have decided to progress on the path of self-knowledge. But if you get into Distancing and Discernment, you will soon create the directional ego of a seeker that will help you to do this work on a permanent basis.

Question: What risks do I face when I work on myself?

Answer: Quite a few because you are getting rid of a conditioning that has up to now for you been the choice of least harm to maintain your inner logic.

Question: Can that be dangerous?

Answer: My dear friend, life is mortal but it is even more mortal if you do not inject some life into your life. Do not forget that the central idea is to get out of this world alive. Truth belongs to those willing to take risks, in other words to those willing to let go of their grabbing points, their systems of belief, everything that makes up their conditioning. Every step towards self-knowledge is a step towards deconditioning. The problem is that the ego will try to recondition itself by using the same steps. That is also true of the religious path, which is why mystics like Lin-Chi and Meister Eckhart have repeatedly told us to get rid of the concept of God. This is equally true of the psycho-analytical process for after a certain time the patient will build an analytical ego that sees everything through prisms that accentuate a cold intellect at the expense of feelings. The ego is an illusion that is constantly searching for new grabbing points. It will do everything it can to keep them. It is the ego alone that is dangerous.

Question: Could you say a few words about Discernment?

Answer: When you are not immersed in your subpersonalities, you can see them functioning. You then have the opportunity to dismantle the logic that draws you into self-condemnation and self-justification as these can bring you no understanding of yourself. For self-condemnation and self-justification do not allow you to go deep enough to the point where you can see yourself as you really are and be sincerely sorry about what you discover. Only if you reach this stage will the lures be less powerful. Understanding does not come from self-criticism or from judgement but from a process of rigorous introspection: "Who says that? Who wants that? What logic directs me? Is it a winning logic? In relation to what is this the choice of least harm? The least harm to reinforce what?" This sharp introspection is, of course, founded on a state of silent observation, Distancing. What the state of silent observation shows you is, firstly, the way thoughts interact, then how these thoughts form into groups and subgroups, your subpersonalities. Introspection will dismantle the link with the fear and guilt that condition you. This deconditioning is the fruit of Discernment and will permit you to develop a new quality of perception of yourself.

Question: How does one reach this new quality of perception?

Answer: The practice of Distancing, closely coupled with Discernment, lies at the heart of the work. As repressed and overcompensated emotional structures, everything that forms the emotional body, come to the fore, little by little conscious energy dismantles these patterns. From this dismantling, allied to a regular practice of silence on an empty stomach, a psychic body, a soul, develops progressively. You will have tangible proof of this in a number of new, more subtle physical sensations such as a feeling experienced between the eyes and an electrical sensation that gradually permeates the body.

Question: So, practically, what should I do?

Answer: The key lies in paying close attention to whatever comes up in your mind. Bit by bit you must build up a part of yourself that does not judge, that reaches no conclusions: in other words a witness, a conscious ego. This will allow you see what you had previously refused to see in yourself. Whenever these emotional layers appear, you must permit their painful memories to rise to the surface. You must let the physical sensations of the repressed emotions come up. To build a psychic body, you must first dismantle the emotional body. Discernment is the sharp tool that will make this happen. As your level of consciousness rises, all processes accelerate. You lose layers of emotional pain that have their own physical reality. These layers resist and protect themselves through various lures, such as emotional outbursts that are completely out of tune with the situation you are in or mental fog that blocks your understanding. But these lures are mechanical. The non-mechanical attention that you will have created in yourself will know how to detect them. It is on the scattered remains of the old emotional body that the psychic body will gradually be built.

Question: I've read your book and I've noticed that, unlike most teachers, you quote many sources of wisdom. Why do you do so?

Answer: To help you understand that there is only one path. That this path has been taught for millennia by awakened beings, that this teaching is not linked to one teacher, and that it is universal. Once you have grasped this, it will help you not to lock yourself up in strange systems of belief.

Question: You mean religions?

Answer: Not at all, as long as you focus on the mystics who, at the origin or at the heart of religions, explored, then taught the leap that leads from the Two to the One, from the dual to the non-dual. But if you use theological constructs erected by generations of clerics, whose principal aim was to provide egos with security blankets, you will set up grabbing points. which will nourish your systems of guilt and fear. By constructs I am referring to purgatory, the Fall, hell-fire, paradise and what have you, beliefs that will maintain your divisions and your unconscious conflicts. Indeed, many people are attached to these systems precisely in order not to let go.

Question: But how can you have a society if you cannot distinguish between Good and Evil?

Answer: Do not do unto others what you would not have them do to you is a pretty good start to social cohesion.

Question: And thereafter?

Answer: Thereafter do unto others what you would have them do to you. Remember that every action must adapt to its circumstances but when the ego entertains ideas of good and evil, we refuse to deal appropriately with the situation we encounter.

Question: Does it help us to be true to a religious code of conduct?

Answer: Yes, as long as the basic attitude is to do unto others what you would have them do to you. Were you to make use of the duties and prohibitions of the Jews, the Muslims and the Brahmins not as a system to reinforce your unconscious guilt but as a reminder to observe yourself, that is to say as a form of Distancing, it could be effective. Unfortunately few religious figures within these established systems get this. To create a personal relationship with God is not the shortest path. From the point of view of the dream of our life, the God of the dream belongs to the dream and supports it. You need to understand this and wake up!

Question: What is sin?

Answer: The only sin is to forget who you are, to forget your real nature. This has nothing to do with the notion of evil that was hammered into you as a child. If you struggle with sin, you will create endless internal conflicts and these will reinforce your guilt and will drive you to harm yourself and others all the more.

A METAPHYSICAL APPROACH

Question: Does awakening means stepping out of time?

Answer: Psychological time is the past. Arising from this past, arising from memory, your identity, projecting itself continuously into a fictitious future, desperately seeks security. It is in the present that the door to awakening lies. To go through it, you have to see with the totality of your being that the present can never be lived.

Question: What do you mean: the present can never be lived?

Answer: Identification with present perception short-circuits it. You superimpose the past or its reconditioned form, the future, onto the present. You need to understand the mechanism that manufactures identifications. Think! Everything that you know is what is perceived. Can what is perceived perceive?

Question: Now I'm really confused.

Answer: Stick with your confusion. Go deep into it. See that you do not exist as a continuous entity. Your true nature is to be found at the heart of the present.

Question: So, how can I find this true nature?

Answer: By avoiding any judgment, any conclusion, for you judge or conclude at the expense of perception. Your true nature lies in the percept, not the concept.

Question: How can I find God?

Answer: Let Him find you! God is nothing more than life conscious of itself, free from all conditioning. All you can do is to create a little bit of consciousness and with it explore your unconscious. You must confront your conflicts, your fears and dismantle your conditionings. Become aware of the tragedy of refusing to flow with the rhythm of a life that renews itself at every moment. You keep attaching yourself to existence via grabbing points manipulated by old pains. Observe how much energy you consume to maintain your armour. Once you have engaged with the practices of Distancing and Discernment and have begun to disidentify from your old identifications, a new energy becomes available. It crystallizes in the spaces that you have opened up. As a result, you feel more alive. Suffering and conflicts quieten down. Next the key questions: "Who am I? Who perceives?" seize hold of you, making you shift into "I am not". Your conscious ego is at last compelled to surrender. It is then that you experience awakening. You are life discovering itself, free of all conditioning. Fear has vanished. The sense of Being, of beatitude, of oneness with everything becomes your reality. You have already had similar premonitions, calling them magic moments or instances of grace. If you manage to get rid of your identifications, Truth at a certain moment will appear by itself. All you need is to stop doing. The rest will happen of its own accord.

Question: So, there is nothing to be done?

Answer: There is nothing to be done for it is always the ego that does. But when in your dream, you dream that you are dreaming, you are closer to waking up. If you develop an understanding of what the mystics and the teachers of different traditions have taught, if you develop a real religious culture, it will, of course, create a series of grabbing points, but these grabbing points will point towards the absence of grabbing points. Read the mystics not to acquire knowledge but to open a field of experience which is your very own. This should be something that happens in the heart of you. Focus on the question and savour the state within which there is no possibility of getting a response and within which your structure loses its support system, its grabbing points. Note how this state connects you to another quality of existence. Feel its energy but reach no conclusion. This process will happen of its own accord. The whole of the universe points towards that.

Question: Who awakens?

Answer: No one. For it is at the very moment that the person disappears, that awakening appears.

Question: Why do various traditions insist on the ego disappearing before enlightenment is reached?

Answer: Quite simply because it is man's destiny just as it is the seed's to disappear in order to become a tree. We are destined to evolve towards other dimensions but to do so we must die to ourselves, to our psychological entity.

Question: How can I become enlightened?

Answer: Be conscious of yourself without attaching yourself to any one thought, and at the right moment your true nature will reveal itself.

Question: Technically, how does this occur?

Answer: One day when you least expect it, fully absorbed in the question: "Who am I?", you will be sent right back towards the totality of your being. Then the question: "Who perceives?" or "What is perception?" will appear. At that point you realize that everything that you know, that you will ever know, belongs to the realm of the perceived. The issue then is: can what is perceived perceive? Awakening, or what you call enlightenement, occurs technically when the energy contained within the question fuses with a concentrated point of being. Unable to seize an answer or a grabbing point, this energy bounces back onto the questioner and dissolves him. The end of the ego is a generalised neural short-circuit which explodes the subject-object dynamic. This is just a matter of reaching the point of critical mass.

Question: I have noticed that many teachers deliver their message from the point of view of awakening. Why do you make the ego your starting point?

Answer: If you haven't been to Australia, you will not discover it if I describe it to you, but it might motivate you to make the journey there. Many teachers have spoken of the state of unity in which they were, but of what use was that to the student? From the perspective of the state of unity, they were probably right. But if you construct an intellectual model from what they say, you will build one more identification and remain exactly where you are. You will construct an intellectual understanding of non-duality; you will regularly read non-dualistic texts; you will develop an ego devoted to non-dualism by imagining that you are part of a spiritual elite; you will identify with the teacher that you have chosen and in your practice you will block yourself in what Ch'an Buddhism calls hazy vacuity, a path where there is a certain degree of comfort, less pain and in which the mind is not sharp, in other words a dead end. Remember that the work is both psychological and metaphysical. To make headway, all you have are your thoughts, emotions, sensory perceptions and dreams. Dig into the layers of your shadow, analyse your dreams and push yourself at the same time in metaphysical questionings, that is to say perturb yourself with questions that make your very foundations shake. You have only a small amount of consciousness available, and a great deal of unconsciousness. Get hold of the 4Ds. They are effective tools. Keep digging in yourself. When you no longer find anything, the task will be done. Of course, your ego will do everything it can to prevent that. The only thing you can do is to train a part of your ego to observe and to dig into itself. Do so and you will raise your level of consciousness. Raise your level of consciousness and you will raise the level of your least harm. But be aware that you are still in your own illusion. One day, through metaphysical inquiry, your ego will trap itself. You will be free and will realize that you were always free.

Question: So, how can freedom be found?

Answer: Metaphysical inquiry provides a fast track to free yourself from your ego, to put an end to your imprisonment. When you are entirely focused on the act of inquiry, when everything that you are can no longer find identification beyond the questions: "Who am I? Who perceives?", you will, at a certain moment, face up to the fact that you are absolutely not. If you can then immerse yourself in that absence, not in an intellectual manner but with the whole of your being, you will find the presence within the absence. This presence is. The mirror that you are has become emptied of you and this mirror reflects life. You awaken in the knowledge that you are life itself. Fear has vanished, desire is dead. Although thought is still present, you use it but it no longer uses you. The old machine that churned out identifications is dead. Freedom is your natural state. It is eternal. Only your imprisonment has a beginning and an end.

Question: It is because I want to awaken that I come to see you.

Answer: You are already in that state, and yet you also want to get there. That's impossible. You cannot find what you already are.

Question: I'm really hitting a brick wall here.

Answer: Study the wall carefully. Work out how it is built and what is it made of. Attack it again and again from different angles. Keep your mind sharp. You have no other tool. At a certain moment it will have become so sharp that it will chop itself off. Trust life. It loves you unconditionally and seeks itself through you. You are the only way it can know itself. And that is why you are here.

Question: You often use similar concepts within the same explanations. Why do you do so?

Answer: To help you understand that concepts are mere grabbing points so that you will attach yourself to none.

Question: I am drawn to the contemplative life. Should I become a monk?

Answer: I do not recommend it. When the seeker is out and about in the world, he has no choice but to face up to his dysfunctions. What he encounters in the world is triggered by what is happening within and this may shake him out of his sleep. Moreover if the monk is not totally dedicated, he may fall into a hazy vacuity, a major lure on the path as I have already told you. That's the reason why Zen monks, while meditating, used to be struck by their teachers with sticks. Originally it was a method that an enlightened being would use at just the right moment, but it inevitably became an empty practice. The world is a perfect mirror. Its drawback is that it excites the mind. But once you have developed the directional ego of a seeker, you will notice that you will progress much faster in the world.

Question: Why do different traditions recommend meditation?

Answer: You have to practice silence for two reasons. To help the evolution of your psychic body, of your soul. And, at the same time, by gaining access to a new dimension, you attain the creativity of a higher order and develop the intelligence known in Buddhism as the bodhi.

Question: How can I open myself up more to compassion?

Answer: By seeing yourself as you truly are and by being profoundly shaken by it. You need to observe the extent to which you are still closed. You need to observe your lack of compassion towards others and towards yourself. Once you see that, the walls you have thrown up around you will begin to fall. You will abandon the system of justifications that you have built to explain away your mistakes, your aberrations. Then, and only then, will you experience the beginnings of compassion.

Question: You are always telling us that guilt is directly linked to the root of identity. Would you say more about it?

Answer: To start off with, you will be in no position to see it as guilt protects itself via a system of decoys and disguises, the task of the unconscious being to keep it hidden. But once you have learnt to observe yourself and others, you will notice the effects of guilt. It generates a system of low self-esteem which is why most people spend so much time and effort trying to seduce others. Guilt colors certain situations, making you think of them as fearful or painful when they are anything but. Guilt also maintains itself through dispersion, fear and conflict, which provide the ego with highly effective grabbing points in order not to let go of its identifications.

Religions have kept this system running for centuries, indeed millennia, through guilt-generating structures that demand obedience to pseudo-divine rules as well as rituals such as the mea culpa which consists in repeating at each Mass "through my fault, through my fault, through my most grievous fault." This guilt was carried by our ancestors, then by our parents who inculcated it into us as children via a set of "You shall nots" when the only valid rule is: "Do unto others as you would have them do unto you". This simple rule, when well taught, can keep a society on an even keel. You can see the workings of guilt when someone survives a crash, escapes from a battlefield or gets out of a concentration camp in one piece; or, to take a recent well-known example, when one of the firemen at the Twin Towers said that with his colleagues dead he felt so guilty at being alive.

The pain encountered during the birth process triggers the first fear which is the ego's fundamental layer. Guilt seems to be the most appropriate concept to define the effects that it has on our life. It is our first major unconscious identification and, like all identifications, it attempts to maintain itself. It feeds on fear that thrives on conflict on the basis that the best defence is attack. Its roots are in the collective and familial unconscious, but its seed is planted at the point of birth when the new-born identifies with the pain of the birth process, which is rarely, if ever, recalled. You see guilt in the two to three-year-old child when an unpleasant event occurs around it. The child is not directly responsible for this event yet will mechanically make a link and take the blame for it. Later, guilt will be very hard to spot as the unconscious will have camouflaged it. Your fears hide it. Question your fears and you will find it. Remember to reinforce your conscious ego continuously through Distancing and to sharpen your Discernment to dismantle your layers of guilt.

Question: Why do we always want more?

Answer: To reinforce identification, of course. The nature of the ego is never to let go of its identifications, which explains its need to reinforce them all the time. That is why the mystics have taught the ascetic path. But if this ascetic path becomes another identification, another grabbing point, it leads nowhere. That is also why the great Ch'an teacher Huang Po, addressing an assembly of monks who had spent their whole lives searching, told them that there was nothing quite like giving up the search. Remember that to let go of identification lies at the heart of the system of the Four Ds.

Question: So the ego will always generate identifications?

Answer: The more the ego is at risk, that is to say at risk of losing its identifications, the more it will produce lures to maintain itself. The weak point of the ego is that it is mechanical. It is not intelligent when it defends itself; it is purely reactive. Through Distancing you have created a less mechanical, less reactive intelligence, an intelligence of a different order. It is this intelligence that will recognize the lures which, once seen for what they are, will lose their power.

We can place the lures in four categories. The first category is when you have made a judgment or come to a conclusion and identify with it. In other words, your intellect has created an identification based on a fixed and critical viewpoint. This is the most difficult lure to detect as we identify with our thoughts all the time.

The second and third categories are the eruption of irrational emotions and of mental fog whose aim is to block introspection. Let's say that you are practising Discernment, asking yourself questions such as: "Who says that? Who thinks that? Who protects what?" when an irrational emotion - anger or the desire to cry - comes up. Or you develop a new understanding about yourself and abruptly forget it. What has erased this understanding is mental fog. Just as a squid diffuses a cloud of ink to protect itself from attack, the ego uses mental fog to protect itself from questions or answers that would put it at risk.

The fourth category of lures can spring up before a sudden rise in consciousness or before awakening. It will be a psychotic event which will often take the form of a divine or a diabolical vision. The seeker's system of belief will manifest this vision to create an ultimate identification, a last illusion, to lock him or her in duality. But if your Distancing is well established, you will see that the ego's defence strategies are stupid, that its logic is purely mechanical. Your ability to identify these ultimate lures will allow you to sharpen your mind, to pull yourself together and to let go of your final identifications.

To summarise, the lures exist to protect the ego, but as soon as they are recognized as such, they will contribute to the process of letting go by showing you where to drill. Do recall that the higher you climb, the more your shadow, your old fears, your guilt will try to bring you down mechanically. Your most trusty safeguard is the quality of your watchfulness, of your Distancing.

You are riding the tiger but remember that it will always try to unseat you in order to devour you.

Question: What should I do when blocked by mental fog?

Answer: You should firstly become aware of it, then bring to the forefront the part of you that is not in its power and keep it there. Your seeker will reconnect and you will be able to pursue your introspection in order to identify and dismantle what blocks you behind the mental fog.

Question: What about during a time of crisis?

Answer: Observe the lures - the tears, the suffering, the anger. By doing so without reacting to them, you will help to destructure the layers of your old emotional body. This will be accompanied by physical sensations. As a result, your directional ego will become stronger. If during these intense moments, the seeker you have developed is sufficiently powerful, the shocks can focus you, sometimes even violently, on the questions: "Who am I?" "Who perceives?" Crises represent excellent opportunities for awakening, for awakening is the ultimate crisis of the ego.

Question: Tell us a bit more about the seeker?

Answer: If you are a seeker, you have developed a searching subpersonality among all your other subpersonalities. You have nourished it with introspection, with silence, with metaphysical inquiry. Reading the classical teachers has sharpened your intellect. You have developed a taste for shaking yourself up with questions to which you do not necessarily have answers. You have introduced a formidable virus into the hard drive of your mind and, when a crisis next occurs, be it large or small, this virus will suddenly gather together the totality of your identification programs, and Discrimination will trigger their erasure. In that moment you will be free.

Question: Why is Discrimination rarely discussed in the West?

Answer: For the simple reason that when we in the West confused thought and consciousness – Cogito, ergo sum – we prevented ourselves from discussing the topic, for it is impossible to discriminate between two things that are apparently of the same nature. Start from the principle that the psychological entity has a mass, that jealousy, anger, fear, not only have energy but weight and density too. As you raise your level of consciousness, you free yourself of these heavy weights which you replace with a lighter mass, less dense energy. The crystallization of your psychic body, your soul, will usher you onto other planes and other frequencies.

The Absolute – God, ultimate consciousness – is not a weight, not a mass, nor a space but the totality of what there is. At a certain moment, personal consciousness, still identified with its residual mass, reflects upon its own nature. Its discriminating reflection forces it to see that it is not the residual mass to which it still adheres. And, of course, as soon as consciousness disidentifies from the body-mind structure, it reveals itself to itself and realizes that it has always been the totality of what there is. That is why oriental philosophies have often spoken of manifestation as an illusion.

Question: Are you saying that Discrimination pushes our defence system to its breaking point?

Answer: In fact, it is metaphysical inquiry that pushes us towards our breaking point and that gathers together our many parts. Think of a game of chess. Metaphysical inquiry plays the game, but Discrimination checkmates us.

Question: Is that when you leave the illusion?

Answer: As soon as you leave the illusion, you will understand that you were never in it. It is only an illusion from the perspective of your identifications which keep it going. From the perspective of the Real, everything is real.

Question: Will you say something about the illusion?

Answer: Using the body or the senses, knowledge or memory, the process of identification with perception creates the illusion that forms the ego, which then creates suffering. Perception is filtered through your psychological entity, or the sum of your identifications. In other words, you only perceive what you think is possible. If today a remarkable number of people are able to walk on burning embers without being harmed, it is because, before embarking on this experience, they had convinced themselves it was possible. It is your memory, allied to your perceptions, that creates your world.

Question: Could you define your teachings in one sentence?

Answer: Certainly. Train yourself to be your own teacher, improve the quality of your Distancing, and keep asking yourself: "What is identification?"

THE TEACHER

Question: How should I choose a teacher?

Answer: To have a teacher is essential. They know their true nature, have recognised the path that has led them there and have shown the obstacles that need to be overcome. If they are authentic, they will never ask you to believe in them. They will show you the techniques that will help you to make inroads into self-knowledge. The more you validate them, the more your confidence in the teacher you have chosen will grow. They should not impose a direction on your life for they know that life itself is perfect and that it will seek out the consciousness of which you form the basic material. They also know that the situations that you have created are fertilisers vital to your growth. While they will urge you to a small extent to modify them, they will not seek to have power over you, nor to lock you up in a system of belief. They will simply provide a mirror which will help you to see what you do not want to see in yourself.

Question: Does a teacher have an ego?

Answer: If you teach, you must have desires and if you have desires, you must have an ego. I know the egoless state and it is void of desire. If there is no desire, there is no desire to teach. That is why a teacher who teaches cannot be permanently in an awakened state. We are all here to make progress, but what must guide us is humility. Remember what the Dalai Lama says: "I too have much spiritual progress to make." Without humility there can be no progress. Without humility, there can be no effective dissolution of the ego and so no knowledge of your true self. You need to understand that if we had nothing more to learn, we would not be on this planet. That is why Buddhism has developed the concept of boddhisattavas, teachers who know the awakened state, yet abandon it to teach.

Question: What does it imply to be a teacher?

Answer: If a teacher teaches, he has an ego with the desire to teach. Where there is no ego, as I just mentioned, there is no longer any desire. The psychological world, upheld by desire, stops.

Remember that the way in which the ego operates is linked to fear and guilt. Awakening has been a death experience for it. After awakening, which is nothing but the ultimate letting go, the ego reconstructs itself out of its basic materials, fear and guilt. To ward off the risk of ever having to let go again, it can set off powerful and destructive losing choices.

Ask yourself why Jesus ended up on the Cross? Was it because he expelled the merchants from the Temple, attacking the society of his time? Why did Socrates create a situation that ended up with him drinking hemlock? Was it because of his permanent opposition to the political correctness of Athens? Why was Hallaj crucified in Baghdad? Was it because he announced: 'My I is Allah. I am God,' thereby provoking the religious fundamentalists of his time? Why was Marguerite Porète burnt alive in Paris? Was it because she wrote and distributed a book that the Church banned? Why have many mystics died in a violent fashion? Was the foundation of their losing choices not repressed guilt? Remember that the raising of consciousness puts the ego at risk and that its task is never to let go of its identifications. The choice of least harm may then be a very destructive one. This is a vital topic that you need to dig into.

Question: What's your opinion of teachers?

Answer: Imagine a city on a plain that generates a high level of pollution. It is surrounded by tall mountains which its citizens never see on account of the haze although, of course, everyone has heard of them. As they never travel out of the city, they seldom think about the mountains. Teachers are mountain climbers who have become guides. Some have reached the summit alone or with a guide and, on their return, have taken student climbers back up to the mountains. The majority of teachers have only read stories of ascents; a few have occasionally left the city to see the peaks for themselves. They can talk about them very well and may have come from a tradition established by a great climber. They are able to attract a large audience but, lacking practical experience of mountaineering, are incapable of leading an expedition. Their teachings will, however, draw a certain number of their listeners towards the heights. Next charlatans of all kinds will teach what they have not experienced, selling a mountain utopia that does not even require leaving the city and where essential practices such as instrospection, immersion in silence and transcending the self are replaced by the individual's subordination to a collective rule, by the belief in the protection of a dead climber, by the feeling of being part of a group of chosen ones.

Question: When I look at you during your talks, I see luminous phenomena. Would you explain what they are?

Answer: Awakening does nothing, produces nothing. It is our fundamental nature. But from the point of view of our illusion, it accelerates the development of our soul. A teacher is someone who, through awakening, has taken his psychic evolution to a higher level. The luminous phenomena you mention are well-known and appear in various systems of belief. Religious paintings of the Italian, Russian and Greek orthodox schools, as well as Buddhist, Taoistic and Sufi iconography often illustrate them. They show that you can build an energetic body in yourself that will allow you to get out of this world alive. This energy of light can manifest on the physical plane and stimulate the transformational process. But do not attach too much importance to it.

Question: Tell us about this energy?

Answer: Once you have built a soul, it can be shown and it can be used. What you see is the energy that will carry my consciousness when my physical body has died. In the psychic worlds, the power of one's presence is linked to the quality of one's absence. An explanation from physics would be that from my point of view there is no observer so what emanates from me, or from my absence, are waves. From your point of view there is an observer and so what you see are particles. It is where these two meet that the phenomena appear. In every case it is better to seek an explanation from science, however imperfect, rather than one that comes from an irrational system of belief, as these might create grabbing points that could be difficult to let go. To advance in the knowledge of yourself, you need to have the attitude of a scientist and trust only what you have experienced.

Question: Sometimes when I look at you, in the midst of the light I catch sight of another face.

Answer: The light you see is a relative reality that comes from the upper levels. You also see superimposed a projection used by your ego to block the transformational processes that are linked to this energy. Once again your old system creates identifications to keep you from progressing. The more your consciousness rises, the more subtle are the lures. Let this energy live within you and feel how it integrates. These subtle phenomena are merely indicators that show that you are progressing on the path. Do not go in search of the miraculous for the less you seek it, the more it will make itself known.

Question: How can I recognize a true teacher?

Answer: Unfortunately the Absolute has founded no schools, runs no universities, awards no degrees. The schools that do exist and that are based on systems of belief have formed remarkable people but they have also turned out quite a few who merely repeat what they have been taught while remaining attached to their pseudo-divine identifications, binding others to their own guilt complexes. They constantly attack whatever puts their identification at risk. They search for power and acquire it by keeping fear and guilt going. In certain cases, they transform their followers into fanatics or even suicide bombers in a bid to preserve their system of belief. It is in your heart that you will suddenly, or progressively, recognize the man or the woman who will act as a guide and who will take you to the summit of yourself. True teachers speak only of what they have experienced and manifest the energy that bears witness to what they are teaching.

Question: What is this energy?

Answer: It is the energy of life. You can see it and feel it.

Question: Can a teacher lead us to the truth?

Answer: A teacher can help you to climb but you can only reach the summit by yourself. Truth has its own energy. It can only be true if you have found it by yourself. Somebody else's truth can never be the Truth.

Question: What do you think of teachers like Eckhart Tolle and Ken Wilber?

Answer: Eckhart Tolle has provided an understanding of non-duality to millions of people. That is very positive. Through his teachings the general level of consciousness has been raised. Once you have experienced 'now', which is nothing else but a good quality of Distancing, you need to learn to use this witness in order to move forward and discover your real nature. As for Ken Wilber, he has produced a metaphysical teaching of great quality that has encouraged many to develop a new comprehension. His contribution has been to sharpen the intellect of a new generation of seekers.

Question: I note that your book is dedicated to three teachers. Would you say something about them?

Answer: I was fortunate in having teachers who never sought to have power over me, nor to have any say over my personal life.

One was a doctor who was part of Gurdjieff's inner circle during his final years in Paris. The other comes from a Tibetan Buddhist background. They have both been beacons to me. But the teacher whose texts sharpened the sword of metaphysical enquiry that led to awakening is Wei Wu Wei.

Question: Isn't what you teach, the Four Ds, a system too?

Answer: Every system is a grabbing point. But a practice of metaphysical questioning, of Discrimination, will sharpen the sword that will one day cut down all your grabbing points. So, yes, the Four Ds is a system but a system that has the power to destroy itself.

Question: You often use the terms directional ego and conscious ego. In what way do they differ?

Answer: The conscious ego is the witness of your life, the directional ego runs it. A good family background, a well-balanced father, a loving mother, a stable society, will as a rule provide the basis on which an efficient directional ego operates in one or several directions, be it in business, in a professional setting, in relationships and in the family. Someone who tries to apply "Do unto others as you would have others do unto you", has already got a directional ego. If someone has a chaotic life and tries to manage situations such as: "I want to succeed in business but keep failing"; "I want to have a home and family but find it hard to commit", it is obvious that he has little or no directional ego. This person will have to build one with a conscious ego which will only come about as a result of silent observation, in other words Distancing. As for Discernment, it reveals the various conflicts within your subpersonalities and their different objectives. The conscious ego, the part of you that does not judge, knows that no subpersonalities are good or bad in themselves. They are merely autonomous identifications linked to life circumstances. The conscious ego's task is to allow them to express themselves freely through it. In so doing, it can confront deeply repressed parts which begin to be dismantled as they come to the surface of consciousness. It is the practice of silence on an empty stomach, together with this dismantling, that will allow us to develop a psychic body, a soul, which will in turn accelerate the transmutation of your shadow.

Question: What do you think of the ascetic life?

Answer: It is fascinating to see what happens when one gives up identifications that are no more than habits. The reason that Bodhidharma stared at a white wall for seven years, that Buddha remained under the bodhi tree, that Jesus wandered through the desert, that Milarepa did not move from his cavern and that St. Simon Stylites stood on top of his column was to speed up Disidentification. The development of the psychic body, of a soul, is a direct effect of this ascetic practice. And yet those who have awakened, who have found the divine or unity, have often warned against the ascetic life or indeed any practice. The point is to let go of the ascetic life as an identification. Vilamakirti said: "There is nothing to be done. Once your false concepts stop and are extinguished, awakening comes." Lao Tse said: "It is through non-action that all is done", and Jesus preached: "Become as little children."

There is no door to awakening. It simply occurs when the ego surrenders all its grabbing points. Any system, any practice, any form of ascetic life, constitutes a grabbing point, of course. That is why when you apply the Four Ds, you need to keep in mind that the game of life is all about letting go. Train yourself to change your habits and see what happens. You do not have to torture yourself any more than that.

Question: How might the creation of a directional ego help us awaken?

Answer: A directional ego will diminish the intensity of the disorder created by different subpersonalities in direct competition with each other. The energy usually employed in dealing with this disorder then becomes available to deepen your nature. Use it to develop your metaphysical enquiry; dedicate at least two or three hours per week to reading the texts of the classical teachers. That is the only way you will create a directional ego keen on metaphysical questions. You will soon discover what a great pleasure it is to shake yourself up with questions that will open new neural connections.

It is when a seeker's directional ego reaches a certain degree of maturity in its introspection and meets the energy available to push it towards metaphysical enquiry that it will see that it has no existence at all. That meeting point is the state of grace.

Question: What's your definition of grace?

Answer: Grace is an effect without a cause.

Question: What does that mean?

Answer: It means that reality has found itself in us. For that to occur we can do absolutely nothing even though it occurs through us, and even though we have to do everything that we can for it. Grace springs up when a powerful will and total surrender fuse together.

Question: How can I reinforce my directional ego?

Answer: By realizing that you hardly have one. By being profoundly shaken at how weak you are and by acknowledging the little love you have to give. By seeing the extent to which you adopt the opinions and arguments of others and those which you encounter on TV and in the newspapers. By recognising how rarely you think and act on your own account. And by observing how often you seek the approval of people you do not even respect.

Question: It pains me to see that.

Answer: Much better to be in pain for a short time rather than to repeat the same old scenarios. When in pain, your Distancing and Discernment will allow you to dismantle the root causes of the problems that you are living. If you do not do that, those root causes that are still active will recreate similar effects and will drive you towards the same old brick walls. Real courage does not lie in squaring up to the outer world, but in confronting what you had previously refused to see in yourself. Only then will you see yourself as you really are and be profoundly shaken by it. Only then will you be able to clean up your act.

Your directional ego is made up of the understanding of your dysfunctionalities. When you have a directional ego that rides your shadow, your life changes.

Question: In what way is a man's ego different to a woman's?

Answer: Man's feminine side, the anima, should be fully developed and in service to his male identity. And a woman's masculine side, the animus, should be fully developed and in service to her female identity. If this is not the case, the dysfunctions linked to the interference between these poles will generate conflicts that will maintain an infinity of grabbing points. Observe your behavior, accept it, understand it and love it for it has been the least harm for you. It is through the acceptance and the understanding of disorder that order arises. It comes from the absence of internal conflicts. Order is what permits consciousness to grow.

Imagine a rocket designed to place a satellite in orbit with a booster on either side. If the force of each booster is not balanced, the rocket will never succeed in its mission. Your masculine and feminine energies are forces that must be balanced.

Question: How can we identify the subpersonalities that form us when we are still identified with our thought processes?

Answer: Firstly, by observing the way in which the same causes have produced the same effects and have brought about the same scenarios in your lives many times. Secondly, by understanding how this happens, what subpersonality produces what effects. This will be achieved through Distancing and Discernment, through constantly asking yourselves: "Who says that?" "Why?" "Who wants that?" "Why?". You will then see your subpersonalities more clearly. You see how they use anger or mental fog when they are at risk in order to sabotage reasoned thinking. You realize that they have an autonomous existence and that they plan, calculate and use lures to keep themselves in power. You also see how they try to maintain suffering in place and how this suffering is the least harm to support the guilt, the fear and the low self-esteem that run the show.

Question: Once the directional ego has been created and the technique of Distancing established, how does it know that it is at the microphone rather than some other subpersonality?

Answer: Through perception. Your evolution runs in parallel with new subtle sensations that are echoed in the physical body: an electrical sensation such as the tingling of the hands and face, a pressure in the space between the eyes, as well as at the top and at the back of the skull. When these are not active, you have shifted into identification and the directional ego is no longer at the helm. It is as if the ignition light on the dashboard of your attention has gone out. These new sensations arise from the conscious ego, the witness, that neither judges nor tries to grab the microphone and that is, and remains, a silent and neutral observer. These sensations are proof of the growth of your psychic being.

The directional ego acts, takes decisions and organises life. When subtle sensations, directly linked to the crystallization of the psychic body, are present and when you are able to respond to whatever comes up, that means that your directional ego is stronger, more stable. You are less dispersed and are moving in the right direction.

Question: The texts say, and you confirm, that there has never been an ego and that no such entity can really exist. Why then create a directional ego?

Answer: For three reasons. Firstly, at a psychological level, the creation of a directional ego will diminish the conflicts generated by subpersonalities in constant opposition. People who succeed in life all have a strong directional ego. A directional ego works best when it has a clear direction. A happy marital relationship, as well as a successful professional life, will reduce unconscious conflicts.

The second reason lies in the fact that the directional ego of a seeker will reinforce the quality of the work. The regular practice of silence and the dismantling of the psychological layers will accelerate the crystallisation of the psychic body, the soul. To experience the life of your soul will diminish your fundamental fear, which is death.

The third reason is that you cannot be unified if the various parts that constitute you have not been gathered together. They can only be gathered together when the directional ego of a seeker has become fully engaged with the process of metaphysical enquiry. "Who am I?" "Who perceives?" "What is reality?" – these are the crucial questions. Remember the story of the many-headed Hydra in Greek mythology? Unless the hero cuts them off all in one go, they grow again and again. This monster stands for the ego, its countless grabbing points, its multiple identifications. Only the directional ego of a seeker, totally motivated by metaphysical enquiry, can gather together all the parts of you. To sever them in one go, they must be gathered together. Only then can the sword of Discrimination cut right through them.

Question: We all refer to ourselves as ' I'. What is this 'I'?

Answer: It is the basic mechanism of identification and the aspect of yourself closest to your true nature. When the 'I' is supported by nothing except its own essence, it can spread its wings, be free, be everything.

Question: How do I get there?

Answer: By being earnest, by introspection, by studying, by practicing silence and by trusting life entirely.

Question: Could you tell us more about this?

Answer: All we know about consciousness is its reflection either of subject to object, as when we are immersed in a love affair; or from object to subject, as when we are absorbed in a problem; or when we are involved in a metaphysical enquiry that focuses us. By unifying us to a greater degree, we temporarily raise the level of our consciousness, making us more alive. Unfortunately we soon fall back into a fuzzier part of ourselves that can in no way open the door onto the Absolute. To keep your mind sharp lies at the heart of the practice.

Question: How can we move from subject-object consciousness to the Absolute?

Answer: The way to do this is to apply acute observation to your thoughts and feelings in order to understand what subject-object consciousness is, what mental reflex-action is, what the mechanism of duality is. This understanding will raise your level of consciousness and will eventually lead to a sudden upsurge, opening up to awakening. It is the process of Disidentification and of sharp metaphysical questioning which together will open the door to your true nature. It is when the subject-object consciousness loses its hold on time that it reveals itself as the Absolute. You get a sense of this between two thoughts. Unconsciously you seek it out when you are involved in dangerous sports. Whenever you find yourself in a high-risk situation, whenever you flirt with death, your connection to time shifts and, briefly, you open up to another dimension. Is it not to get closer to life that you seek dangerous situations?

Question: What is consciousness?

Answer: Consciousness is what permits reality, the Truth, the Absolute to become aware of itself. Reality, the Truth, the Absolute is what does not change. Subject-object consciousness, reflex-action consciousness, maintains an illusion of movement and of the passing of time through identification. It is when this illusion is exposed that consciousness and the Absolute coincide.

Question: What happens at that moment?

Answer: Our vision of the world, based on the idea of a universe existing in time and space, crumbles. We are no longer in that universe; it is the universe that is in us. We are pure consciousness. We are what we never ceased to be.

Question: How does consciousness perceive?

Answer: Consciousness does not perceive. It is pure perception.

Question: Would you explain this further?

Answer: When the perceived object and the perceiving subject have both disappeared, there is nothing except a blissful and limitless perception. Consciousness – life – then rediscovers itself. But the most surprising aspect of the situation is that when you experience this state, you realize that you were always in it. At that point you understand that you are eternal. And as what you are is not born, it cannot die.

Question: That's reassuring.

Answer: Who does this reassure?

Question: I see what you mean: there is no such thing as a person.

Answer: Remember that the word person comes from the Latin persona, which means the mask that Roman actors used to wear on the stage. There is no such thing as a person, there has never been any person and there never will be a person. But to know that now is of no use to you as you can only set a part of your person to work on your person until the mask falls off.

Question: So who am I?

Answer: The body is perceived, then the mind which perceives the body is perceived, then the witness which perceives the mind. Where this witness cannot be perceived is where you are.

Question: At times I want something and at other times something else.

Answer: The nature of mental processes is to be divided and to maintain division.

Question: What you're saying doesn't get me anywhere.

Answer: The only person who can help you is you by training the small amount of consciousness that you have to explore your unconscious with courage and determination. Life, the divine, has planted within you a seed of the Absolute. As an infant you were once intimately connected to this seed which was not conscious of itself. To protect your vulnerable child against the world's aggression, you built an armour. This armour created the conflict between what you want and what you don't want. You must explore it for by doing so you will dismantle it. This will free up energy and will allow you to build a directional ego and a soul. The result will be that you will be much more unified in what you want.

Question: I can see that, but I also know that no desire will ever fully satisfy me.

Answer: Only your true nature will still the uninterrupted flow of your desires.

Let us recap. Distancing and Discernment begin to break down your armour, permitting you to identify better your fears and guilt. Once you have built a conscious ego that accepts every part of yourself, all your subpersonalities, two aspects will come to the fore. First, a directional ego that will be in charge of your life, if your education and history had prevented you from having a strong one. Having acquired one, you will experience fewer conflicts in your choices and you will become more unified and courageous. You will know how to say yes and how to say no. You will see situations much more clearly because you will have dismantled most of the prisms that colored them.

At a higher level, you will build a psychic body, a soul. Through the gradual dismantling of your psychological armour, of your old emotional body, the conscious energy of life will irrigate the seed that you carry within you. You will feel your psychic body develop and will have the physical sensations that belong to its growth. Cultivating these sensations in silence will open you up to new dimensions. One day, at a moment when you least expect it, you will be unified by the right question and will face up to the fact that you are absolutely not. Only then will you be free of all desire. Remember that on the path, the more you develop yourself, the more you are likely to be helped.

Question: Helped by whom?

Answer: By the winged parts of yourself for as your psychic body develops, it comes in contact with the higher realms of the psychic world. Angels, who are mentioned in every tradition, are conscious energies of light living in other dimensions. The more you are in contact with these dimensions, the greater the help you will receive from them. As soon as the psychic matter your soul is made of has crystallised, the raising of your consciousness has begun. Ultimately you are the totality of what there is. You are not in the universe, the universe is in you. As you evolve, your response to your inner and your outer worlds shifts. As a result, other dimensions will have more access to you to help you. You have felt this when, free from doubt, everything went your way and you manifested what you wanted whether it was getting out of a seemingly impossible situation or finding the right person with whom to share the rest of your life.

Question: The books I have read on positive thinking advise me to keep repeating: "I want money, I want success".

Answer: If you do what these books tell you, the energy of life will send you back the message: "I want money, I want success". This will merely materialize the wish, not the wished-for reality.

You must think and act as if this reality had already come into being. Many of the books that deal with the subject, among which the best-seller 'The Secret', offer a certain number of keys. For these keys to work, you must have the right lock, and that means to be unified which implies to have solved your inner conflicts, your inner contradictions. For that to occur, you must get rid of the false securities that keep you on the surface, and must free yourself more and more from your deep fears. If you want things to change, stop thinking and acting as you do. Practise the first two Ds earnestly and you will soon reap results. There is no reason why you should lack, apart from your insistence on carrying a deadweight of fear and guilt. By digging into them and by being above them, you will gain access to a much more abundant life.

Question: How should I practice positive thinking?

Answer: Begin by saying; "the divine, life, the universe" – call it whatever makes most sense to you – "is sending me love, success, money." You may find that easier to accept. Affirmations do not work if they only express what you believe at a superficial level. They work if you are unified. They work if you know that what you want is already there. The energy of life does not cheat. Everything is already in the eternal present. Understand that there is a natural order with which you are unified, or not. You have grasped that consciousness is energy. If matter and consciousness are energy, everything at the heart of unity is possible. Quantum mechanics shows that the observer has an effect on the observed. What we call miracles are natural phenomena linked to other levels of consciousness that science has not yet found a way to describe. Who is the ultimate observer? At the level at which you find yourself, you can see that there is not a thinker on the one hand and a thought on the other for the observer is the observed. Discover who you really are. Keep the fire of your practice burning. Only your true nature will deliver you from fear and desire. When you are everything, you want for nothing. Aim for awakening and the remainder will manifest in its proper place.

Question: Could you discuss how our ego blocks us?

Answer: Fear makes us say no to what is. It is linked to pain which relates to the body, while suffering relates to the mind. Pain means that the body is in need of attention, that it is at risk. Similarly, suffering comes from the fact that the individual entity, this seething mass of more or less repressed memories with which you identify, is at risk from change, at risk of losing its grabbing points.

Question: Could you go into this a little deeper?

Answer: The wise who have tapped into the energy of life accept everything that is. They know that the grass is never greener on the other side. The ego's fundamental mechanism lies in its refusal to accept what is and to project something else instead. This mechanism has the rejection of the pain of birth as its origin. You have perhaps observed how two year olds – the infamous terrible twos – structure themselves on denial and how they resist any change. Suffering and fear stem from attachment to habits, from resistance to change and from the refusal to go with the flow.

Question: How can I be released from fear, from suffering, from the misery of the world, and find God?

Answer: Understand that fear, suffering and the misery in the world are in you. Your internal conflicts have created them. You have little ability to act on the outer world, but with courage and determination, and by practicing the first two Ds, you can begin to dismantle the suffering in yourself. From this dismantling, the psychic body, the soul, will be born. As your level of consciousness rises, your understanding of God will change. At a certain moment you will let go of everything. You will cease to maintain a grabbing point that is ultimately nothing more than a projection of yourself. You will never find God but will allow life to know itself in the empty mirror that you will have become. That is the state that Buddhists call awakening, Hindus illumination and the Christian and Sufi mystics God or Unity.

Question: My problem is that I suffer a great deal from fear and anxiety.

Answer: Grasp that the ego is nothing more than fear management and that it works through a mechanism that flees pain and through a compensatory system to avoid dealing with it. When fear attacks you, it is an opportunity to study it live. Fear and anxiety come from repressed emotions and are lodged in your body. Ask yourself whenever the sensation of fear arises, "Who is afraid? Which part of me is afraid?" You will soon discover that behind the fear there is a lack of confidence, and that behind that, there is repressed guilt. You should observe it but not conclude anything for were you to do so, you would support an intellectual system which would provide you with one more escape route, and that would solve nothing. So, explore fear. Let it live in your nervous system. If you can taste the electrical sensation of fear that circulates throughout your body, you will see that it is neither pleasant, nor unpleasant. It is just electricity running through your nervous system. By accepting it, you will dismantle your anxiety. Remember that when you identify and accept the lower layer, the one above it loses its power. Get rid of anxiety by accepting the physical energy of fear and your life will soon improve for you will see your situation as it is rather than through the prisms of anxiety. Thereafter your actions will be more appropriate to what you encounter and you will enjoy greater success.

Question: You're saying that what really worries me is the fear of fear?

Answer: When you fight something within yourself, you always reinforce it. What maintains the ego is the escape from fear. Let us imagine that a man fears that his spouse will leave him. Everything that reminds him of that possibility translates as a physical sensation, that is to say the movement of the emotional body through the physical. Once he has identified this sensation with fear, he will look for an escape, for another grabbing point as fast as he can: this will usually be in the form of food, sex or work. You must see how this functions but without drawing conclusions. It is true of everything that frightens you: the loss of your family, of your money, of your health etc. The ego is a fortress that has been built to escape from fear. Explore it for that is how you will dismantle it.

Question: How?

Answer: Through the use of silent listening.

Question: What is that?

Answer: Silent listening - Buddhist mindfulness, the position of the Witness - is Distancing, a mental technique that, properly applied, allows you to see your thoughts move. Until you have seen them move, you have accomplished nothing.

Question: I'm finding this difficult.

Answer: Develop your attention so that it encompasses the visual, the auditory fields, the weight of your body and unify them. That, as you now know, is Distancing. After a while you will be able to witness at a distance your thoughts and feelings in motion. You will note with increasing clarity that you are merely mechanical, that you act very rarely, that you mostly react. Your system creates fear and this fear is the least harm to maintain your identifications. Why does the movie business produce so many films that stimulate fear? Because your identity is addicted to fear. You feed what you wish to flee and by doing so, you hang on to the same old grabbing points.

Question: What should I do about my fears?

Answer: Your psychological structure has built itself to escape fear. This escape is an attempt to control it. Fear creates suffering. You need to accept it in order to understand it. Experience the physical sensation of fear without naming it so that it can move about freely. Do not let your thoughts take over. Stay with the physical sensation. Observe it, but draw no conclusions. Do this and your mind will sharpen, will become stronger and more alert. At a certain moment your mind will recognize that it is not this repetition of fear and of anxiety based on guilt. It will see that it is not memory supporting the system through thought. It is then that this emotional magma will really begin to dismantle. It will no longer nourish fear. Naturally, by raising your level of consciousness, you will not wander off in the train of thought that set it off.

Question: I often feel crushed by anxiety when I wake up in the morning. What should I do about it?

Answer: Realize that the psychological entity holds you in a permanent subject-object dynamic. See this and accept the fear and anxiety that inevitably accompany it. Experience the physical sensation of fear without compensating by trying to escape from it. By compensating I mean: thinking of something else, phoning a friend, raiding the fridge. Observe the sensation and let it flower fully within you without labelling it with the concept of fear, without becoming caught up in some mental association. You will soon notice that fear, as I keep telling you, is nothing more than an electrical sensation that runs through the nervous system.

If you let the sensation play itself out without naming it, it will lose its negative or unpleasant connotations. It is simply a neutral electrical sensation. See the reality of the mental mechanism that feeds itself by naming fear or by wandering off in various thought associations. If you really see this, you begin to experience a new perception which expands through space. Your consciousness is now moving above fear, above its shadow. Grasp the nature of your mental identifications in order to let them go. Keep practicing and you will soon wake up in a happy frame of mind.

Question: What is the origin of fear?

Answer: Pain, guilt and violence. But, first, I want to focus on violence. We live on the planet of the apes. We are the most violent species on the planet which is why we dominate it. This violence terrifies us. To deal with it, we have developed a psychological entity, our ego, the result of thousands of years of evolution, of thousands of years of confrontation with violence. This ego must maintain duality and to do so it is vital that it never lets go of identification. Humanity adds up to seven billion apes determined never to let go of their identifications. Their basic economic imperative is to grab bananas from other apes and to climb the tree of the ape hierarchy.

This inevitably leads to violence which we try to avoid by running away from it. Society has been built to limit this violence and to offer us systems of escape, linked to our social status and purchasing power. The moment we think that the lack of money will make us lose our position in the hierarchy, anxiety immediately attacks us. Let us learn how to let go. Let us become wise. The wise feel no fear for they have gone beyond the ape stage and are no longer violent.

Question: I fear the future and this creates terrible anxiety in me. What do you suggest I do?

Answer: Fear conditioned by the past produces anxiety. Running away from anxiety will determine your future. If you want this to change, you will have to have the determination and the courage to confront your fears, to face up to the situation in real life that you want to avoid. Change the way that you interact with the world. On the battlefield that is you, observe yourself, question yourself, push introspection. You will see that your fears are fictitious. You will rapidly dismantle what blocks you. True courage is to face up to what you do not want to see in yourself.

Question: I am aware of my lack of generosity.

Answer: You cannot be truly generous as long as fear possesses you. Once you really understand this, everything will change spontaneously.

Question: How do you explain depression?

Answer: Depression is a mechanism that reinforces grabbing points whenever these fail and it is, as always, the choice of least harm. Where does depression come from? Generally from loss: the loss of someone close to you; the loss of love; the loss of money - bankruptcy or ruin. Post-natal depression stems from the loss of the identification with the pregnant state. Remind yourself that the nature of the ego is never to let go of its identifications. When life forces you to let go of a set of identifications, the ego will recreate other grabbing points. Freud is clear about how melancholy appears when there is a loss of libido.*

Question: You say that we attract everything that happens to us. I lost my father at the age of twelve which had a terribly destabilizing effect on my life. I surely did not trigger that?

Answer: We attract everything that happens to us. If we do not take that as a given, we will never be able to dig deep within ourselves and dismantle the primary causes that make us do what we do. Mechanically, the program of going towards the pleasant and avoiding the unpleasant will generate the lure that it is somebody else's fault, be it father, mother, brother, grandfather, destiny, karma, the will of God, or whatever. How will you apply this to your own case? Understand that while you are not responsible for what happened to you, you are responsible for what you have done with it. Of course, you did not cause the death of your father but you must take responsibility for your actions and reactions to it. If you consistently make a link between your present crisis and your old drama without going deeply within yourself, you could drift from one crisis to another. By staying on the surface, you block yourself and pave the way for the next crisis. You always attract what happens to you. Understand the part of you that gains the most from the crisis, from the past. Let it go and be more alive.

Question: I am soon to be married to a lovely man but I am feeling undue pressure from him and his family to leave my religion and to convert to his.

Answer: To convert or not is ultimately your choice. You are right to show loyalty to your religion. It is the cultural context in which you were born. If it is not too recent a religion, you will find in it texts written by mystics who experienced the leap from the Two to the One. Sharpen your mind by reading what they wrote about the experience of awakening. Do not forget the etymology of the word religion. It means: that which links. The more you practice silence, introspection and read metaphysical texts, the more you will create your own religion. Transform belief into experience. Move from ready-to-wear to become your own designer and clothe your being in a body of light.

Question: To me, life sometimes looks like a tragedy.

Answer: Life is a tragi-comedy. The more evolved you are, the more you see it as a comedy, the less evolved, as a tragedy. Why do Chinese Buddhas burst into laughter? Because they see life as pure comedy.

Question: What does faith mean to you?

Answer: Faith is a profound conviction that leans on doubt. A part of you has faith, a part of you has doubt. It is by exploring doubt that you will strengthen your faith and that doubt will diminish. As a result your faith will increase. This exploration must be based on reason for it is reason that should guide what you test in yourself. Your faith will grow through those tests. And never forget that it is enlightened reason that makes you tolerant.

ORIGINS AND ATTITUDES

Question: We all know we are going to die. Could you say something about death?

Answer: Everything changes all the time and at each and every level, be it the atom or the cell. All organic forms die, but your real nature, which lies above the mind, neither dies nor changes. The ego, however, searches for continuity via unceasing mental movement. It has to maintain its identifications, its belief systems at all costs, including the Resurrection of the Dead, reincarnation, the Last Judgment etc. All belief systems are compensatory responses to fear. By investigating the foundations of fear, you will open the door to life. Your real nature was present at your birth. The ego is what you have accumulated ever since. You need to challenge yourself with all your might. Use the sharp steel of this questioning to cut the mental knots that form you. You will then see that death, like awakening, is the end of your mental habits, and that the end of your mental habits is just like the end of a dream.

Question: I'm afraid of death.

Answer: Be one with life and you will free yourself from death. You must tear off the mental mask that, through its system of identifications, has made you take yourself for your body. Once this identity has been torn off, you become life experiencing itself through the body. You are no longer your body. You are life itself and life does not die.

Question: What happens before birth?

Answer: At long last a real question! Stay with it.

Question: So what's the answer?

Answer: Distancing and Discernment will help you let go of your identifications. Inside the space that you have created in yourself, the practice of silence permits your soul to grow. When the substance it's made of reaches critical mass, a crystallization process will occur. You will then have a conscious vehicle which will provide you with a non-conceptual answer, an energetic answer. This will be a partial answer to the question. The complete answer can only come from your own total absence. Cross that threshold and you are free. From the perspective of this state, there are no effects as causality disappears in awakening. But from the perspective of the soul, awakening is a fantastic accelerator of its growth. It represents a real leap in its evolution. Later, with increasing ease, the soul will find its real nature, unity.

Question: Where does reincarnation fit into this?

Answer: Think of a bulb and of the electricity that lights it up. The bulb lights because the filament gives off heat. When the filament has been used up, the bulb dies. You could imagine that the memory of the bulb would incarnate in another bulb, but that does not make much sense. Your real nature is to be the electricity, not the bulb. It is not the electricity that lights up: it is the bulb. But it is through electricity that the whole thing happens. As the mystics say, God does nothing yet it is through Him that everything happens.

Question: But isn't reincarnation a reality? The Asiatic traditions certainly seem to think so.

Answer: Let's go into this topic a little further. If, at the point of death, the soul has not transcended the four dimensions – three physical, one temporal – it will aspire to continue its evolution. But that cannot be the memory of a given individual who would reincarnate in another individual. To develop a psychic body, you must maintain yourself above your thoughts and feelings, above your imagination. There is no such thing as continuity of memory. Free from psychological memory, the psychic body, the soul, may, if it wishes, pursue its evolution, that is to say fully realize consciousness beyond the four dimensions that support its own illusion.

Question: How do you see karma?

Answer: Karma is nothing but your birth. Your parents, genes, social milieu, nationality, the culture that envelops you, are all contained within your birth circumstances. You carry your parents' psychic energies, having absorbed them as a baby and as child. To be free of one's karma is to take the best of those energies, to transcend them and to let go of the charge of fear and guilt that accompanies them. It is written in the Brahma Sutra, the foundation of Hindu philosophy, that whoever frees himself, whoever awakens, frees his lineage. Free your self and you will free your lineage. Your children may even love you for it!

Question: You tell us that awakening is triggered as a result of a real question. So, what is a real question?

Answer: A real question is one to which there is no easy answer. This question is a focus of energy. If it is a real question, it is a focus that creates an opening in your neural net. You are now building a diamond with no impurities. The more the motivations behind the question are psychological, the more you deal with your shadow, the more you deal with what is repressed, the more impurities you are clearing. If the question is metaphysical, it is powerful and relatively free of impurities. The answer, or the absence of an answer, may then dissolve you. Freedom lies in that dissolution.

Question: What role does free will play in all this?

Answer: As fundamentally there is no ego, there is nobody to make any choice. Free will is dependent on memory. In the early stages of conscious development, there is almost no free will. Unconscious energies throw themselves onto the stage of consciousness and seize the microphone. Little by little your directional ego forms through education and working on yourself. This is where free will becomes a reality. You are now the conscious creator of your choices between good and evil, between "I should do this, I should not do this". The more the directional ego is built, the more strongly anchored the notion of free will become. Next, as you evolve, your directional ego turns increasingly into the directional ego of a seeker. It becomes progressively subtle. It chooses less and less. Increasingly it is the situation that dictates action. The ego becomes the witness of the processes that unfurl before it. It is at this level that the question of free will becomes a subject of metaphysical inquiry. "Who chooses what?" "What is the nature of this 'I' that chooses?" When you engage fully in these questions, you find the very essence of free will.

Question: Is there such a thing as destiny?

Answer: You have not one but thousands of potential destinies. Imagine a translucent cube floating in a black and starry sky. On one of the sides of the cube there is an entry point, your birth. From this entry point, a line leaves which divides into thousands of others and heads towards the other side of the cube where there are just as many exits. According to the choices you make, you move from one line to another for they are interconnected. Ride the best possible lines of your destiny! Whether they are winning or losing depends on the choices that you make and on the logic that drives them. When you get to the other side of the cube, what you will regret above all will not be the bad things you did, so much as the things you could have done but did not do. So live to the full. Put life into your life. And make sure that you are on the best possible trajectory.

Question: What should a seeker's attitude be towards life?

Answer: To have no attitude.

Question: But don't you tell us that the seeker must search?

Answer: To search is to take risks. It is to leave the comfort zone of your psychological compensations, of your adherence to the system of beliefs with which you have identified. To search is to raise your level of consciousness. This implies entertaining doubt, uncertainty and, above all, challenging yourself. That is the way you let go of your identifications, and that is the heart of the search.

Question: I find the hypocrisy that I meet in society and in people hard to handle. What should I do about it?

Answer: Hypocrisy stems from the opposition between the inner self-image that you want to maintain at all costs, and the outer self-image that you project onto the world. The greater the difference between these two self-images, the greater the hypocrisy.

Now look at your external self-image. If you observe yourself, you will see the amount of energy that you expend to appear handsome, intellectually brilliant, seductive. The world may then send back to you a reflection that will consolidate the internal image, which is based on fear and on low self-esteem. It is the nature of the ego to be hypocritical for it is fundamentally a thief which, through its various identifications, steals each perception for its own use.

Question: So who am I?

Answer: The body is perceived, then the mind which perceives the body is perceived, then the witness perceives the mind. It is there that physical and psychic sensations meet. It is there that you can taste a new energy. Stay there as long and as often as possible. There is nothing else to be done. Stay with the one who perceives, not with what is perceived.

Question: I've heard you say that 'I' is nothing more than thought identified with itself. Could you explain this?

Answer: Thought has created the 'I' through the subject's identification with the object: you, the subject, and what is other than you, the object. This 'I' lies at the origin of your world, which seems as real as the corridor of perspective that you create when you place one mirror opposite another. But if you remove one of the mirrors, the perspective collapses. In much the same way, the

'I' as subject maintains itself because it has an object. The subject cannot exist without an object, just as the object cannot exist without a subject. They are as interdependent as the corridor of perspectives is on the two mirrors.

Now think. The subject, as soon as it is conceived as subject through the act of conceiving it, becomes an object. The act of conceiving a subject turns it immediately into an object. Therefore the subject can never be conceived. If the subject cannot be conceived, where is the object?

Question: What you say destabilizes me.

Answer: You cannot see what you are. You can only see what you are not.

Question: How should I deal with this?

Answer: Experiment on yourself by using the following practice. Begin by trying to understand what 'I am' means. Then let it go all of a sudden and drift along with the sensation of being. Just stay with it. Then again come back to 'I am' with a strong desire to understand what it means. Let go once more and again find the sensation of pure being without superimposing anything onto it. Practice this well and you will feel an opening and a compression of space in yourself which blends in with external space. Do not stay stuck in an intellectual understanding of what I have told you. Make it practical. Keep exercising. One day you will see that what you are has never begun. It is only what you are not that begins and ends.

Question: What's your take on space?

Answer: Space is perceived by the body. Disidentify from your repressed structures within the body, and your tactile sensations will grow in space. Next, at the heart of your psychic life, a brand new space will expand within you. The more you can navigate through this new space, the more your understanding of your identity will evolve.

Question: What about time?

Answer: All we know is the past. It projects itself on the present and conditions itself as the future. When we see something, our conditioning identifies its form. Our memory gives the thing a name. This identification with name and form creates the world as we know it. This world shapes the repetitive patterns of our thoughts, a major part of our emotions and creates our desires. We live in an imaginary world that springs from our projections. The future comes from the conditioning of our memory. The present is continuously stolen by the mechanism of our identifications, by the mechanism that makes us superimpose, using names and shapes. In the eternal present, our dimension of time past-future is contained. But in our dimension of time the present can never be lived.

Question: What role does memory play in the awakened state?

Answer: It is a memory entirely free of self-images. It is a purely functional memory. It is no more than a toolbox. From this memory, thoughts spontaneously arise in tune with your situation. Thought is then just a tool. It is no longer our identity.

Question: Can you tell us what triggers awakening?

Answer: Consider the hydrogen bomb which is made up of two components: on the one hand plutonium, on the other a sophisticated explosive device. It is the impact of the detonation of this device on the plutonium that will set off a chain reaction. Awakening is the explosion of the ego. The plutonium in this image stands for the metaphysical inquiry for which you have developed a taste. By developing a taste for abstraction, by challenging yourself with questions to which there are not necessarily any answers, you have refined this plutonium. It is there, waiting – just like all the other aspects of yourself linked to food, to sex, to money – waiting to seize the microphone, to have access to consciousness. As for the sophisticated explosive device, it represents a psychological crisis born of introspection.

One day, through the constant application of Distancing and Discernment, an old structure, an old emotional layer, will be dismantled and this will generate a crisis. As this crisis will be new, it will force you to focus on a powerful question. The metaphysical subpersonality that you have kept going and refined through reading the classical teachers and challenged with acute questionings will seize consciousness and trigger the explosive device of the crisis. It is the confrontation of the two that will destroy the ego. It is because the crisis will be new that the energy of the questions: 'Who am I? Who perceives?' will be new too, and that can only work if memory does not interfere.

Question: Why have I not awoken?

Answer: Because your mind is topsy-turvy as a result of what you have not sorted out in yourself. Being identified with the management of yourself, you are self-centered when there is no self. You keep looking in the wrong direction, for the inner and the outer are not where you think they are.

Question: Is awakening sudden or progressive?

Answer: In 7th century China, the Fifth Patriarch of the Ch'an School decided to choose a successor by offering the post to whoever wrote the best poem. The most intellectually brilliant monk in the monastery, Shen Hui, penned this verse: "The mind is a bright mirror on a stand; / Take care to wipe it all the time and allow no dust to cling." Everyone in the monastery was sure that he would win. In response, Hui Neng, an illiterate monk who worked in the kitchens, dictated the following verse to one of his fellows. "There is fundamentally no stand of a mirror bright. / Since all is empty from the beginning / Where can the dust alight?" Of course, Hui Neng won the competition, but this caused such a scandal that he had to get away from the monastery as quickly as possible or would have been in great danger. That is how the School of the South, also known as the School of Sudden Enlightenment, was born, in contrast to the School of the North that had adopted a progressive path.

Only metaphysical questioning, by making you move away from what is false, can help you to integrate your real nature and that occurs in a most abrupt fashion. You must understand that you are absolutely not and that the point of departure is 'I'. 'I' can no more know itself than the eye can see itself. The eye sees itself through the use of a mirror. 'I' knows itself through the use of the object. For 'I' to awaken, it must disappear, following the disappearance of the object. Only then is 'I' revealed as the Absolute.

Question: What are the greatest obstacles on the path?

Answer: In Ch'an terms, the first obstacle is hazy vacuity, that is to say states of mind in which the intellect is not sharply engaged. Even more dangerous is the second obstacle, the fossilization of a non-dualistic understanding into an intellectual system. To combat the first obstacle is very simple. Whenever your awareness diminishes, get up, walk around a little, then return to your practice. To conquer the second, challenge yourself with questions that shake your foundations. When you do that properly, you experience the physical sensations of your emotional body moving about within your shadow because it has been put at risk by the question.

Question: How do you define thought?

Answer: Thought is double-edged for it both frees us and binds us. Consciousness has been fed for thousands of years by fear, conflict, struggle and strife, and we live life from birth to death as separate identities. Very rarely do you question this identity. If you do reflect on it, you will see that your identity is built upon the thoughts that you identify with. I am short, I am tall, I am a man, I am a woman, I am white, I am black, I am American, I am Chinese, I love this, I hate that. Thought as you live it is generated by identification and is entirely in its service. It arises from experience. It is consciously stockpiled by memory where it becomes knowledge, and by the unconscious which will use it again and again to provoke similar experiences. Thought is our identity constantly seeking continuity. For most people thought is consciousness: I think, therefore I am. This is fundamentally false for it is no more than the mechanism of identification maintaining itself through thought. It is essential to realize that thought has a physical reality. It consists of electricity running through your neural network. Thought, a subtle material, entraps being in the net of opinions, beliefs, reasonings, images – all of them identifications. Once you understand that thought has a physical reality, it is possible to empty your brain of its conditioning. Discrimination, thought properly used in the process of metaphysical inquiry, triggers the neural short-circuit which allows that to happen.

Question: Why is man violent?

Answer: We are built on a bedrock of pain: the pain of the birth process, of the shock that moved us from the fish-foetus stage to that of the infant mammal. This repressed pain has conditioned fear and guilt. From that moment we are in duality, we are in conflict for when there is you and others, there is likely to be conflict. We have developed a mental system based on the management of fear and guilt which makes us escape in conflict and violence. This mental system has become our identity. It has brought us to the point where we dominate the planet. Our ego has been built on the control of fear and violence.

Question: How can we break the cycle of violence?

Answer: By acknowledging that it is in us and by understanding its origin. We are built on a violent act – the birth process – that is all the more so as its memory has been repressed. Our parents and our teachers imposed on us the world-view that they inherited from their own parents and teachers. A world-view that most of the time gives considerable value to violence, to force and to domination. This indoctrination through the history of our country, through the movie industry, through the press, has seeded violence in us. We have been educated to become a member of a nation by being reminded of the victories that the tribe with which we have been taught to identify has won. The priests of the established religions have also invented all manner of sins to control us through fear and guilt. This has forced us to repress our own nature, and that too has triggered more violence. We now say that we want to live in a non-violent world, but what part of us really wants that? And how big a part of us is it? Why did Jesus teach us to turn the other cheek? To de-activate the cycle of violence, of course. Only a choice as shocking as turning the other cheek could make a mind surrender its grabbing points.

Question: So, what should I do?

Answer: Just be aware of what is around you for it is your situation that always guide your actions. Never be the prisoner of a strategy. As the situation changes all the time, a strategy should not be fixed. If it is, there is a strong likelihood that it will be subject to fear, and that it will be a losing one. If you are not drowning in your own projections, you can begin to dismantle the root causes that activate them. As fear has generated violence in you, you project it onto others and that triggers the response: I better attack before the others get me. Conditioned by religion, you have repressed a part of your sexual nature and have constrained your behavior. What has been repressed will always express itself in a destructive manner. At the same time you must face up to what you have not dealt with in yourself otherwise you cannot become free of what binds you. Religions have created an object – God – of which you are the subject, to which, in other words, you have been subjected. Thereafter the function of organized religion has for the most part not been to encourage you to integrate your divine nature, but has limited itself to structuring society. After 2,000 years of warfare, the Judeo-Christian religions have produced the Western model of society. It has brought us the Rights of Man and democracy. It is an open and tolerant model that, in spite of imperfections, has come up with a civilization that tends towards a lessening of violence.

Question: How can you speak of a lessening of violence when ever since September 11th we have been thrust into a more violent world?

Answer: You need to grasp that September 11th is the latest in a long line of war-like episodes that began in the 7th century A.D. in Arabia. A religion is always the reflection of its Founder. There is no doubt that Mohammed experienced unity. One can feel the intensity of his mystical experience in the Koran. But by the time the text has reached the surahs of Medina, the enemies of the Prophet have been turned into the enemies of God. Mohammed was both mystic and warlord. The strength of Islam is that it successfully integrates the various aspects of man's nature in its system of belief, which explains its extraordinary expansion. Man, as I have already said, is the most violent species on this planet. Mohammed's original contribution was to channel this energy and transform it into a holy war – the jihad. Unless Islam is understood in its mystical dimension, as do the Sufis who realize that the jihad is not an external battle but an internal one, it cannot dismantle this violence. Look at the Islamic world. Many of the countries in North Africa and the Middle East are still ruled by dictators, kings and emirs who wield enormous power. It is no accident that a transcendent God to which our lives are subject and who holds our destinies in His Hand is reflected in the person of an all-powerful king or leader. We in the West took centuries to go beyond this logic before we were freed by the Enlightenment. Modernity, education, the emancipation of women, the economic success of the West have put the building blocks of most Islamic societies at risk. When Bin Laden spoke of crusades, he was living the logic of that long line of war-like episodes. Let us hope that the Muslim world finds its path towards democracy and that Islam encounters its Luther and its Enlightenment by rediscovering the wisdom of the Sufis.

To survive, we must go beyond the Darwinian logic of the competition between species. As a result of this logic, man dominates the planet. But this dynamic has taken such deep root in him that it has translated into a death struggle within the species. We need to make a quantum leap in consciousness for by doing so we will abandon systems generated by fear and guilt reinforced by theological aberrations. The reason that the concept of a law-making God keeps growing is because it still fits our present evolutionary stage. It allows men to dominate women. It encourages man to be an alpha male and the more he dominates, the more violence he exercises. While religions have provided societies with the opportunity to structure themselves, today they are often more destructive than constructive. The concept of a tribal Creator is bad: bad for women, bad for human rights, bad for peace. It was fatal for the World Trade Center. It stimulates guilt which nourishes fear which, in turn, generates violence. We need to develop a global metaphysical vision based on what unites us, not on what divides us. A thorough knowledge of the texts of the mystics of different traditions will take us in that direction. God does not speak. How can unity, the Absolute, divide itself into a speaking subject and a listening object? Only the awakened speak and thereafter their disciples build a religion. If the aberration of a God in man's image were abandoned, there would be no more suicide bombers killing thousands in His Name, nor would there be leaders with a hotline to Him. To put this madness in perspective, remember that Nazi soldiers had inscribed on their belts: 'God with Us'.

Question: You say God does not speak, but was it not God who transmitted the Koran to Mohammed?

Answer: Certainly not! Mohammed was a sage who knew that the One is not divisible which is why he announced that Gabriel had transmitted the Koran to him. Out of the three Abrahamic religions, Islam is the one best suited to help metaphysical development. Awareness, for example, is protected through the ban on alcohol. Idolatry is prevented by the ban on images of God. The absence of clergy, at least in Sunni Islam, stops the institutionalization of a central power structure, the only authority being the Five Pillars that must be respected. These comprise the statement that there is no other God except for Allah and that Mohammed is His Prophet; five calls to prayer that punctuate the day; being charitable towards the poor; submitting to the fast of Ramadan; and, if possible, making a pilgrimage to Mecca at least once in one's life. It is also important to realize that there is not one Islam but several, and that these have only the Five Pillars in common. The Islam of Andalusian Spain and of the Sufis was open and tolerant as this was the Islam of Ibn Arabi and of Rumi respectively. The Islam of Malaysia and Indonesia are equally open-minded. It is apparent that climatic conditions have had some influence on Islam. The problem today is that the Islam that is rising in power is Wahabit. It comes from a desert people, it is medieval and is neither open nor tolerant. Islam promoted a culture in the 7th century that corresponds to man's nature. Mohammed the mystic was also a warlord for the world in which he operated demanded that he take up arms against his enemies. The social structure that he erected was nonetheless a leap forward, which is why it flourished and spread so fast. Let us not forget that during the 11th and 12th century, Arabic science was the most developed, for in Islam reason and faith are separate. It is probable, for instance, that had Galileo lived in Andalusia, which at the time was governed by the Moors, his discoveries would have met with no resistance.

Question: What do you see as the biggest change in human evolution over the last fifty years?

Answer: It is neither globalisation nor is it the progress in information technology and mass communication. It is how we relate to pain. We no longer suffer the way we used to. Consider the pain our ancestors had to endure. Think of toothache, the difficulties of childbirth, the agonies of dying, all without anaesthesia.

In the industrialised world, our rapport to pain has been through a major shift. Religious beliefs attempted to diminish pain through its acceptance. They were the choice of least harm in our management of pain. While in Asia karma explains our present-day pains in the light of past misdeeds, we Christians in the West carry the burden of original sin. We endured centuries of thinking: "God is putting us through this pain because he loves us. It is because He wants the best for us that we, miserable sinners, are going through such miseries." In these religious systems, guilt is used to justify, accept and manage pain. Today we suffer less and less. For at least thirty years we in the First World have been beyond the experience found in Genesis 3:16 that we should be "cursed to give birth in pain". Today more and more women in the West give birth without pain through the use of the epidural.

We keep inventing new molecules to deal with physical and mental pains. One result is that the old religious systems of justification have become progressively obsolete. But do not forget that they bore pearls of rare worth: the writings of the mystics.

Question: Why do we destroy nature?

Answer: The problem is that man's level of consciousness is out of synch with his technological level. Man has not changed but his technological capabilities have. It is not a question of man and nature as man is part of nature. Do not contrast the one with the other.

At the height of the Roman Empire, for instance, lions disappeared from North Africa because of the voracious demands of the circus. We are also told that the inhabitants of Easter Island destroyed their world when they cut down trees to move the statues of their gods. We will only stop damaging our environment once we have raised our level of consciousness, once we have grown away from an anxiety conditioned by fear that makes us seek escape in extravagant consumer-based compensations. The higher the levels of consciousness to which we aspire, the more we will be in harmony with what surrounds us.

Question: How can we rid society of racism?

Answer: The root cause of racism is the fear of what is different, what is other, what is unknown. This fear puts our system of identification at risk. Thereafter we reject the other by projecting a negative judgment onto him and the other then becomes bad or evil. The other will only represent good if we can identify with him. What does our system of identification towards good or evil rest on? On the collective systems of the tribe we belong to. What characterises them is that most of the time they maintain fear and guilt, the conflict between good and evil. The revealed religions – Judaism, Christianity, Islam – are partly responsible for our neural conditioning. They all propose a Creator on the one hand, leader of the forces of good, and on the other a Devil, primary agent of the forces of evil. The more radical the followers of these religions are, the more closely identified they are with their moral code, the more many of them will be intolerant, racist, homophobic.

This is understandable as their identifications are put at risk by what is different. The demonization of the other, of the stranger, is present in most cultures where it every so often makes violent appearances. You have seen the conflict between Hutu and Tutsi in Rwanda, between Hindus and Muslim in India, between Chinese and Malay in Malaysia, and in many other countries too. Racism will only disappear when we decondition ourselves by disidentifying from archetypes that nourish fear through the conflict between good and evil. It is by bringing our level of consciousness above the seething mass of fear and guilt that the other, the alien, the unknown will be accepted. Not accepted merely on the surface as a result of political correctness, but fully and truly accepted because we will have let go of our fear-based identifications. To open our heart we must ride our fears.

Question: Don't you think there is a difference between the guilt that arises from the trauma of birth and the feeling that the individual has as a result of unacceptable actions?

Answer: It is the nature of the ego, which is a nonentity, to keep its own fiction running. This fiction rests on the first identification with the painful process of birth and the fear that springs from it. This identification, the first important neural imprint, will be the ground on which guilt, reinforced by culture and education, will develop. This fear, this guilt, our basic identification, will, like any identification, seek to maintain itself. Why do you under certain circumstances feel compelled to misbehave, to depart from what should be the golden rule in society: do unto others what you would have them do unto you?

When you behave in a cruel, nasty, selfish manner, the guilt that lies at the base of your ego is always being nourished through a system of lures. These lures, your aggressive subpersonalities, will apply a logic to justify their behavior. These aggressive subpersonalities are the choice of least harm which will feed the levels of unconscious guilt. You can see that when, after the energy of these subpersonalities has been expressed, a sense of guilt appears.

Question: What do you mean by that?

Answer: Remember the last time you behaved badly with your parents or your children; when you locked yourself up in an irritability that made you say things you later regretted. How did you feel then?

Question: Is there such a thing as legitimate guilt?

Answer: As you want to justify a protective barrier that you call legitimate guilt, why not observe the behavior of society based on it? Above all, it brings fear: the fear of punishment, the fear of God, the fear of having behaved badly. Now ask yourself: what does fear produce? Violence, of course.

Question: I'm referring to a simpler kind of guilt. I was supposed to visit a friend in hospital a few days ago but in the end I did not go and felt bad about it.

Answer: You are talking about a feeling that relates to the preservation of your self-image. Your image's stability was at risk and this feeling was the least harm to maintain it.

Question: The next day I brought him a present, so didn't my guilt turn out useful?

Answer: To maintain your self–image, you generated a compensatory action that restabilized you and that may have made your friend happy. In that sense it was useful. You live in a world in which you compensate and overcompensate all the time in order to set up an equilibrium which nonetheless eludes you. Dismantling the logic of your compensations is the essence of the work on yourself.

Question: You tell us that guilt is universal. But in China and Japan, there does not appear to be any guilt in the attitude to sex.

Answer: The attitude to sex in the East is very different from what you experience in the West. In Japan, for example, one taboo bans the showing of pubic hair on television. Look at the way guilt pervades oriental societies. Why does shame regularly generate suicide there? Why in China when people say: "Everything is going well. I am very happy", do they often quickly turn to the gods and the spirit worlds and say the opposite: "I am in very bad shape. Business is going really badly," when it is doing perfectly well. The issue is to avoid upsetting the gods, the spirits, to avoid attracting their jealousy. Why do Asiatics think that unless they burn fake money or luxury goods made of paper once a year and send the fumes into the thereafter, they will upset their ancestors and bring calamity down upon themselves? What are these systems of belief founded on, if not on repressed fear and guilt? Study the Mayan civilization, which used to sacrifice thousands to obtain the protection of the gods. Or the Shi'ites who ritualistically flagellate themselves to commemorate the death of their leader, Hussein. In certain African, South American and Asian countries people also go through physical pain to purify themselves or to safeguard their communities. Unless they inflict physical torments on themselves, these men will not occupy the best places in the group's hierarchy.

See the way that systems of fear and guilt surge at the conscious level. Individuals suffering from obsessive compulsive disorders may wash their hands thirty or more times per day. They will count the number of steps they take or the objects in their immediate environment and will latch onto whether these are odd or even, interpreting them as the triggers of good or bad luck. These disorders also lie behind the constant reading of cards or the use of divinatory tools to search for a combination that might bring peace of mind.

At another level, look at the mechanisms that make us strike a bargain with a superior entity, pleading with it that if we commit ourselves to doing this or to give that up, it will give us something in return. Such behavior patterns stem from systems of repressed fear and guilt and are the least harm to keep them running.

As soon as the shadow no longer has you in its grip, things change. A good case in point is beginner's luck. Because a part of you is brand new and is not yet linked to the old system of fear and guilt, your winning parts can then express themselves freely.

All casinos know the phenomenon of a rookie gambler winning a great deal of money at the tables. Remember that guilt is simply the most appropriate concept to define the effects that the shadow has on your life.

Question: How would you define your teaching in a nutshell?

Answer: See what you do not want to see in yourself.

LOVE

Question: Everyone is looking for love. What can you say about it?

Answer: You cannot know love until you have totally reconciled yourself with yourself, in other words with the parts of you that you do not love. Otherwise what you call love is a projection that can all too easily turn to resentment or to hate according to which part of you is affected by the other's attitude. You need to think this through as it is a critical issue: does love exist?

The closer you get to your real nature, the more the quality of the love that you experience will resemble love. The most perfect love that the ego can give is the love of a parent towards a child. It is because the father or mother wholly identify with the needs of the child that this love feels like real love. Why do you run after love? Because love gives off the scent of your real nature. Unconsciously, your yearning for the Absolute, in which you wish to dissolve, draws you towards this scent. The more you raise your level of consciousness, the more you are unified, the more your ability to love improves.

Question: What do you mean by the ability to love?

Answer: Once free from your old fear and guilt patterns, you do not have to spend so much time managing your dysfunction and so are less taken by compensatory behavior. The result is that you can give more attention to those close to you. Love is a gift of one's self that comes from self-forgetting.

But if the attention you give to another stems from the fear of being abandoned or from any other projection, it is not love. It is by realizing how little you truly love that you will be able to love more. Decondition yourself and your ability to love will increase. Get into a real dynamic of change, and you will no longer want to change others but will accept them as they are. Only then can you begin to love them.

Question: How do you see relationships?

Answer: Relationships provide first class opportunities to further one's self-discovery. See how you idealize your partner, admire in them aspects that have been repressed in you, yet also accuse them of characteristics that you yourself display, but cannot accept. The other person is a mirror. Use it. Practice Distancing and your partner will inevitably bring up situations in which you will can deepen your Discernment.

Question: Is there such a thing as an ideal couple?

Answer: Yes, and it will need to harmonise on five levels. The first level is the physical in which sexuality will evolve as a game whose purpose will be the other's pleasure.

On the second level, the psychological, the couple's neuroses will either be compatible or not at all. For instance, they will broadly agree on everything or argue about petty details. As a rule, it can take several weeks to see whether things will work out.

The third level, the intellectual, will be stimulated by a common culture, a love for travel, music, art. Here the couple will share a freshness that will provide the opportunities for the relationship to renew itself and last.

The fourth level, the worlds of the soul, needs time to be achieved. The partners will feel the other's state of mind in their absence. As they evolve, their souls will learn to fuse, to separate, to fuse again. This is the level on which they will dance with the gods.

The fifth level requires a philosophical and metaphysical vision based on a shared experience of awakening, of freedom, of a full integration of the goal of life. This is a theme beautifully illustrated in Hindu mythology through the love stories of Vishnu and Lakshmi, Siva and Parvati.

When these five levels are operating, the couple's harmony fully resonates. You need to tune them just as one would tune an instrument. To build a happy life together, the minimum a couple requires is to strike a common chord on the first three levels.

Question: What about love and passion?

Answer: Passion expresses your primary need to fuse with life. This does not stem from your real nature but from the illusion that makes up your identity. At the heart of this illusion is your vulnerable child. The amorous state – passion, romantic love – is its attempt to recapture unity. We all know people who keep falling in love. Unconsciously, they are seeking unity. The repetition of patterns that engender failure will unfortunately maintain suffering and it will in turn maintain vulnerability. Everything that is in us is desperate for continuity.

Question Is falling in love a mistake?

Answer: Not at all. When you are drawn towards your partner, your emotional body vibrates in tune with the freshness of the situation. This freshness temporarily masks your repressed layers, which are linked in each of us to our history, to the energy of our mother, of our father that we have integrated and rejected at the same time. As long as these remain unactivated, we experience a scent of unity. It is that scent that draws us towards our partner.

As the relationship unfolds, the unresolved elements rise to the surface and dissipate this scent. By constantly observing and questioning ourself, our partner will be a mirror we can use to see what blocks us.

Question: Are you saying that falling in love is a good thing?

Answer: Stop thinking in terms of good or bad. Ultimately whatever happens to you is positive. Try to understand the logic that drives you. You have everything you need to grow in your immediate entourage, everything you need to see yourself and to move above your shadow.

Question: Does love have a place in awakening?

Answer: Awakening is pure love. When you are one with everything, you are love. Your psychological entity is an armour that allows you to confront what is other than you. When the armour falls away, there is nothing but love. Think of a cinema screen onto which a film is being projected. The film is your psychological entity unfurling its own story. The screen is your real nature veiled over by the film made up of all your identifications. Opposing pairs – good/evil, war/peace, love/hate – write the script of your film. Your real nature is to be the screen. It is never affected by the film, yet without it there would be no film. The moment you discover you are the screen, you are life that loves itself.

Question: Can we experience love while we are in the illusion of the film?

Answer: The more you dominate your fears, the greater will be your capacity to love. Your ego is nothing but the manager of your fears. As such the love it gives is always a compensatory love. Open yourself to love again and again. Whenever you say I love you, and feel yourself carried on the waves of love, your real nature appears in the depths of you.

THE SOUL

Question: What is the nature of the soul?

Answer: The soul is an intermediary stage in the raising of subject-object consciousness towards reality - which is that which does not change - a stage that opens onto psychic worlds. The physical body evolves on the physical plane: the psychic body, the soul, on the psychic plane. The one does not necessarily contain the other. This is a major deception that the monotheistic religions have perpetrated. You don't doubt that you have a physical body. For the psychic body it is the same. The moment you have developed a soul, you will know it for sure.

Many traditions have discussed this topic, yet people know so little about it. In Hinduism and Tibetan Buddhism, Tantric practices and those of kundalini, both closely related to energy, have been codified and used for the development of the soul. Jesus in the parable of the talents spoke of it, as did Mohammed in his teachings. In the Secret of the Golden Flower, Taoism provides a manual for the crystallization of the soul as does Gurdjieff in his own way. In the oldest tradition, the Egyptian, it is the union of the ba – the most developed spiritual aspect – with the ka – the conditioned aspect – that will produce a more or less developed ka. But we should go no further into these complexities as they often do not help. While the writings of certain mystics contain nuggets of gold, these are partly lost in the sand of religious systems of belief.

Let us now look at how the psychic body evolves. Our vulnerable child* is connected to our essence. It carries the seed of the development of the soul buried beneath the layers of our identifications. Through Discernment, we gradually destructure these layers of fear and guilt and free ourselves from jealousy, aggression, shyness and so on. As we let go of our grabbing points, we feel our old emotional body vibrate and open up. We become aware that we have shed a weight. Once we have disidentified from these old structures, we open up to a mental silence of a better quality that will attract other energetic frequencies. These will accelerate the dismantling of the repressed emotional body. After some time, having made a sufficiently large stockpile of subtle energies in the spaces we have freed up, we will feel an electrical tingling running through our body, as well as physical sensations at the top and at the back of the head and between the eyes. They bear witness to the way in which the higher energy is transmuting the lower energy that has been dismantled through Discernment. Practice the techniques that I have taught you and in a few months you will experience these sensations.

They are the physical evidence of the development of the subtle substance that makes up the psychic body and that cannot be dissolved by death if the process has gone far enough. It is quite simple: all you have to do is to practice introspection and regularly sit in silence for that is the fastest method to develop your soul. Understand that the psychic body belongs to the next stage of the illusion. Maharaj and others told us that, in their own quest, they met Gods and Goddesses, but that they were of no great interest. What matters is freedom and freedom is beyond physical, psychological and psychic conditioning. If you develop a soul, you will be alive on another level, you will be less fearful and that will weaken your ego. The result of awakening, of enlightenment will be the acceleration of the development of your psychic body. Finally, with this psychic body you will learn to dissolve in unity.

Question: What should I do to develop my soul?

Answer: The worlds of the soul are made of space, light, information and energy contained within consciousness. Science today teaches us that matter and consciousness are energy. It is within ourselves that we are going to develop our soul through the use of energy.

Let us imagine a series of Russian dolls made of tinted glass. The smallest is the darkest – which is where most of us are now – while the one that contains all the others is the most transparent. To help your soul evolve, you will have to learn to transfer energy from the lightest doll to the darkest which, little by little, will become clearer.

You have noted that the first part of the work is psychological and have carried it out through observation and introspection. Correctly interpreting your dreams has also sharpened your Discernment. By partly dismantling your repressed structures, you have created a space in your psychological laboratory. The work and the practice of silence have opened up connections from the darkest of the dolls to the next one up. You can feel this through a tingling between the eyes, at the top of your head and in the electrical sensations that run through the whole of your body.

From now on everything is going to go much faster. You will learn how to open up to the energy of the next bigger doll in order to assimilate it. You will use this energy to accelerate the dismantling of the darker dolls – your shadow. During your meditations you will learn how to adopt an attitude that will simultaneously be both active and passive. You will identify those parts of you that resist and that are blocked. These are located in your body: remember that psychological problems are always translated by a physical sensation. You will learn to surrender to this superior energy which will dismantle your shadow structure and will transmute it bit by bit into a body of light. By doing so, you will move progressively from terrestrial archetypes to cosmic dimensions. Archetypes are nothing more than psychic structures made from our beliefs. Your true nature is to be the biggest of the Russian dolls, the one whose light is infinite and which contains all the others.

Question: You explain that to develop my soul, I must open myself up to a higher frequency of energy. Is there any way I can accelerate the process?

Answer: To open yourself up to other energetic frequencies, you need to practice silence on an empty stomach in a state void of thought. That is how you develop your soul.

For several years, I used to sit in places linked to an archetype of Christian energy. As I was living in Europe at the time, these included the great cathedrals as well as the Basilica of Santiago of Compostella. When you practice silence in a place where for centuries millions have connected through prayer and worship to the same archetype, you will, if you are sensitive, feel this higher frequency.

The Wailing Wall in Jerusalem is especially powerful and in London the Chapel of St Faith in Westminster Abbey is energetically charged. In Asia there are many places such as the Temple in Kandy, Sri Lanka, which contains one of the Buddha's teeth. Imagine the energy that Mecca accumulates given that several hundred million individuals turn towards it five times per day. Objects can also be energetically charged. In the Royal Ontario Museum in Toronto, there are two interesting Buddhas while in the Guimet Museum in Paris jade prayer discs act as psychic gateways. Certain artists, after experiencing a breakthrough in consciousness, can transmit this through their work: the Korean Lee Ufan has produced artefacts that open onto another dimension. The right attitude is to connect to the energy while remaining as free as possible from their archetype, from the system of belief that supports them.

When you visit these sites, it is as if you are plugging yourself into a psychic grid. Give it a try. It is fascinating. Remember to trust only your subtle physical sensations. Watch out for your imagination as it may try to intervene by using the psychological aspects of the archetype. To be entirely free of thought in these venues is key.

Question: Is it possible to awaken without having a soul?

Answer: Of course, through shock or at the point of death because the brutality of an event can strip away the personal entity, forcing you to let go of all your grabbing points. Awakening is your natural state. It is always there and appears as soon as the ego lets go. The ego is what you have accumulated, nothing more. After awakening, the ego will reconstitute itself according to the level of disidentification that it has attained. The psychological fragments that have not been properly discerned will reassemble according to their common characteristics, and the ego will be rebuilt. Until consciousness has moved from the shadow, where identifications with fear and guilt lie, it will take itself for the mind. To unravel your identifications is the preliminary work that will allow the crystallization of the soul.

Question: So we need a soul to evolve?

Answer: It is part of the process of man's growth. But to work on yourself purely to build a soul would be misguided. You should work on yourself to know yourself, to understand life, to know the divine. You need to discover what psychological motivation makes most sense to you now. To know the divine seems to me the best aspiration for it is the most powerful archetype, or at least it was for me.

Question: So who has a soul and who hasn't?

Answer: It is not because you are born that you are psychically alive. Everything, as I have pointed out, is linked to evolution. Ten thousand salmon roe end up as three or four adult fish. Thousands of acorns may yield one oak tree. Out of two hundred million sperm, two hundred will manage to cross the fallopian tube but only one will fuse with an egg. Among several billion individuals a fraction will be psychically conscious and a fraction of this fraction will awaken. This planet is a factory for the production of consciousness. Unfortunately the factory today is in pretty bad shape. You may find this deplorable but everything is evolutionary. At this level, there are no Rights of Man.

Question: I get what you're saying but it still angers me.

Answer: How often do I have to tell you that anger protects fear, fear protects guilt and guilt, linked to the original fear, keeps the whole system going? See it! This teaching is progressive, but it can also be abrupt. It is all down to your character. As soon as you see the full scope of the false, the truth appears. You have always been the truth. Your conditioning is a bad dream. But the dreamer can work on the dream and make it better. The dreamer can also act consciously on his dream life and change it from within. That is one of the things that the soul can do. But what the dreamer should do above all is to awaken for that is his true vocation.

Question: Would you tell us something about the psychic worlds, the world of the soul?

Answer: There is no point in doing so and it might even block your progress.

Question: What do you mean?

Answer: Do not use your imagination.

Question: But...

Answer: If I spoke of the psychic worlds, you would generate an image and it would block you. To refrain from imagination is critical. Otherwise your imagination will create an illusion of the psychic world in which you will see yourself travelling, inventing past lives to explain away your present-day issues. If you have not mastered your imagination, how do you hope to travel through the psychic dimension? The essential work is the practice of silence on an empty stomach. If you cannot stop your train of thought, get up, take a few steps, then return to the practice which is a good quality of Distancing. Whenever you have a psychic experience, be it visual or auditory, forget it or you will use it as a grabbing point.

Modern physics has shown us that the observer has an effect on the observed. The more the observer is conscious that he is the observed, the more the psychic entity will evolve and the more effective it will be in those worlds. But when those experiences occur, do not identify with them or they will become another escape route, another system of identification. Freedom is not easy to reach on those levels if awakening has not already occurred.

The gate to freedom will first open through such questions as: "Who am I?" "Who perceives?"

Question: Could you say more about the nature of the soul?

Answer: The soul bathes in perception. We live in a world of thoughts and words. Words are explained by other words, thoughts associate with other thoughts. Everything is linked to memory, which functions by association. Perception does not function through association. The more the soul evolves, the more its perception widens. For man at the beginning of the 17th century, the sun rose in the East and set in the West, which meant that the sun went around the earth. By the middle of the same century, the great astronomer Kepler, using a primitive telescope, showed that the opposite was true: it is the earth that circulates around the sun. Today through the use of orbital observatories, we have greatly enhanced our perception of the universe. The nature of the soul is to be both the subject and the object of perception. The soul opens onto fields that are more and more vast. It does not function through association. Its vocation is to dissolve in the All. The soul as object returns to the ultimate subject, the ultimate perceiver, the Absolute.

Question: What do you mean when you say that the soul is both the subject and the object of perception?

Answer: At the start of its evolution, your soul is your object of perception. This allows you to see energetic fields, auras, the world of the archetypes. Then, as the soul grows, it is a subject pursuing its cosmic evolution, but a subject that has integrated the fact that the observer is the observed. Finally, the soul as object is drawn towards the ultimate subject, the One into which it dissolves.

Question: You say that the psychic worlds are real.

Answer: Their reality is relative to the consciousness of the perceiver. Within this consciousness, a psychic body which can perceive the psychic worlds has formed. This is the next level of evolution. It is not the freedom that we are seeking but a path that can lead to it. As a rule, an evolved psychic entity will be more benevolent, compassionate and powerful. But it can also be dark and evil. Freedom is never at the level of a psychic entity, no matter how refined. To work on oneself, to practice silence, will crystallize a soul, a psychic body. A stage in the evolutionary process will thereby have been crossed.

Through its own experiences this soul will know that it is no longer linked to a physical body. This will diminish the ego's basic fear which is death and therefore weaken it. It is important to remember that freedom can never occur within duality. In the most developed levels of the collective unconscious, you are still beset by an illusion. But from this level of the illusion, it is a lot easier to let go of it and to learn to dissolve in ultimate reality, in the very essence of life.

Question: What are the powers of the soul?

Answer: If you want to experience the powers of the soul, you must work on yourself psychologically. Accompany that with the practice of silence and you will crystallize a psychic body. This may lead to the development of siddhis, in other words to psychic powers. These include the stimulation of the intuition, the ability to see auras and energetic fields, to leave the body and to act on the subtle planes, namely the potential and the virtual. It involves the ability to ascend to the light of superior levels, such as other space-times like the worlds of the Platonic Ideas. It also includes access to the world of symbols, of the collective unconscious and to what Jung calls the archetypes. This provides an opening onto worlds that have their own reality, that exist at the limits of the manifest and the non-manifest and that are supercharged with data.

Although the siddhis are proof of progress, many teachers consider them an obstacle on the path. They appear because the ego has mutated, has become more porous, more subtle. It has changed its level of consciousness. But if your motivations are not pure, if you have forgotten that the siddhis belong to the mental world, if you identify with them and make use of them without Discernment, you may fall into an even more opaque form of identification. This may also provoke severe psychological, even physiological, disturbances.

If you do not tap into the reality to which you aspire, you will have the greatest difficulty progressing towards your ultimate goal: which is freedom, unified consciousness, nirvana, the Kingdom of Heaven. To sum up, you could say that before awakening the siddhis act as a brake on your evolution, but that after awakening they find their natural place.

Question: What about the evolution of the soul?

Answer: The nature of the soul is to be between time and reality. If awakening has occurred, the soul will find its path towards reality with increasing ease for it knows that what is never becomes and that what becomes never is. A truly evolved soul knows how to let go of becoming in order to be absorbed by being.

Question: What happens when you die?

Answer: Death is the ultimate letting go. It provides an opportunity to reintegrate your real nature if you have already awakened while alive. If you have not done so, it represents your last chance saloon. You need to understand that psychological identifications impregnate the psychic matter that has accumulated throughout your life. Phenomena linked to your memory may then appear and send you down the wrong trail. These phenomena will condition the dream of the after-life in the psychic dimensions. This dream will relate to your systems of belief, among which are found the Tibetan bardos, the equivalent to the heaven and hell of the monotheistic religions, and the Happy Hunting Ground of the Great Plains Native Americans, in other words what populates the archetypes of the collective unconscious. When you come into this world, you have the potential to crystallize a diamond to get out of it alive. It is up to you to develop it. If the day you die, this crystallisation has not gained sufficient substance, everything will dissolve in the collective unconscious. But when your soul reaches a certain power level, you leave the archetypes of this planet behind and your psychic destiny becomes cosmic.

GOD, GOOD AND EVIL

Question: You often speak of the Absolute, but rarely of God. Why?

Answer: If you consider that God is external to you, you turn Him into an object and therefore create a powerful identification. You will only find what you call God once you have abandoned all grabbing points. But as that puts you at risk, you prefer to maintain more or less peculiar systems of belief in order to remain in duality, in other words to hold onto your psychological entity. Remember your real nature: you are everything, the One, the Absolute. When you entertain an image of God, of awakening, of any kind of security, you cut yourself off from what you truly are. The Truth is for adventurers for they are the ones who take the risks to abandon their comfort zone.

Question: What does God mean to you?

Answer: The energy of life has created us. Why call it God? We were brought up by our parents. Why create a parental substitute that reproduces reward and punishment? Our fear conditions us to desperately seek security. We then invent a God who decides for us. This concept leads us to think: "I am in God's hands." "It was God's will." "God bless my nation." God is a concept onto which you project the sense of safety you so desperately lack. It would be more helpful to think of God as a glass whose contents would change in line with the raising of your consciousness. Be courageous. Lose your grabbing points. Change the contents and, one day, empty the glass for good. Once empty, it turns into the Absolute. It is then that the energy of life recognises itself as such.

Question: Doesn't God tell us to sin no more?

Answer: For Heaven's sake, God does not speak! The Absolute is consciousness of life itself and this consciousness is One. How do you expect this consciousness to express itself in duality? How can God the subject talk to an object which He cannot be! You need to think this through. It is when we are told that God speaks that trouble begins.

What would you think today of a man who had been told by an inner voice to take his young son to the top of a mountain and sacrifice him because that was God's will? A man who, just as he was about to kill his child, heard a voice ordering him not to carry this out as God had simply been testing him? A man who, having come down the mountain, saw a bush which burned but which was not consumed by the flames? You would probably expect him to be carted off to a psychiatric ward and his son immediately removed from him. The examining psychiatrist would almost certainly conclude that he was suffering from a psychotic disorder. Yet it is on the base of this myth that the Abrahamic religions were built.

This myth became central in the definition of a Chosen People, an Only Son of God, a Single Prophet.

You are still living in the madness of those systems and can surely see their destructive effects today. Note how you move into attack mode whenever you feel your system of identification is at risk. Attempting, and generally failing, to obey pseudo-divine laws stimulates the guilt at your base. This leads you to repress your sexual urges, dietary desires and behavioral leanings. Inevitably this repression feeds your guilt, delivering you into the hands of religious clerics, who are often only religious in name. Next in the name of religion they relieve you of the sins they created in the first place. Repressing your true nature is bound to increase your instability. Note the craziness of it all.

The only sin is to forget your self. If you are drawn towards religion, read the mystics of the various traditions. Develop a real religious culture, a culture based on the sayings of those who have awakened, and you will see that it is they, and they alone, who speak. Practice silence and introspection and you will understand that the sole person against whom you have really sinned is yourself.

Question: What do you make of evil, of the devil?

Answer: The devil is nothing but the manifestation of the energy that says 'no'. From a theological point of view this is true given the devil's rejection of God. It is also true of the rejection of your first identification with the pain of birth. This is the first cause of your mask of fear and guilt which promotes the evil from which you wish to flee. Naturally, in so doing, you feed the process. In general the more one is evil, the more one suffers, and the more violent one is. And the more violent one is, the more one suffers and the more evil one does.

When you pray to God to deliver you from evil, you refuel what you are trying to flee. If you project human qualities onto

God by saying that: "He is good, compassionate, all-forgiving", you are upholding a set of polarities that can only exist in relation to their opposite. Without God, no devil. Without a devil, no God. Think about it. That is why the Buddha spoke of the Middle Way, which means not falling for identification.

The moment you let go of the subject-object dynamic, you are the Absolute, and the taste of the Absolute is the divine. Objectify it and you create the concept of God. You then fall back into duality in which everything exists in relation to its opposite.

God is all there is except an object which is what awakened teachers have been telling us for thousands of years. Remember Lin-Chi's phrase: "If you meet the Buddha, kill him!" In a similar vein, Meister Eckhart, preaching to a congregation of nuns, said: "My sisters, it is high time you got rid of God!"

To shed a little light on this, let me tell you about the priest of the Parish of Ars, a village in the center of France. A great Christian saint of the 19th century, he achieved a high level of Disidentification. As the period is not that far removed from us, we have many eyewitness accounts of the miracles, or what we might call unexplained physical phenomena, that happened to him. In his quest for God, this good man would regularly confront an obstacle that he called the Devil's hook. On certain nights the Devil would attack him and in the morning the priest's body would be covered in bruises. There are even reports that speak of kitchen utensils flying towards him and harming him. As the priest was very developed psychically, his ego, to maintain itself, created a demonic manifestation that fed itself through this struggle.

There is no other Devil than ourself. The demons of the different traditions are nothing more than our repressed subpersonalities. They can occasionally generate a psychic reality that can manifest on the physical plane. It is always about us, never others. It is our belief systems that determine what happens to us and these evolve according to our level of consciousness. Man's true worth lies in his decision to go beyond his condition, a worth that leads him to see that this condition is the result of his belief systems.

Question: I see evil in me. What do you advise me to do about it?

Answer: Well done. It's good that you've become aware that we are all a mixture of light and dark. The more you deny the evil in you, the more you reinforce it. The more you allow it to invade you, the stronger it becomes. Once again, everything will depend on the quality of your observation. Imagine that you live in a ten-room house. Choose one of the rooms and put your devil in it. It can do whatever it wants in this room but cannot get out of it. This is the way to deal with it.

If you do not do that, if you refuse to acknowledge its presence, if you repress this part of yourself, it will gain power and invade the whole house. Be aware that when you feed it, it will never have enough and will try to take full possession of the house. So allow it the free run of that room and put it on a strict diet. Observe this part of yourself, understand its logic and little by little it will lose its power. The more you progress in the understanding of yourself, the more secure you will be.

Question: You say that God cannot speak and cannot be an object, but surely God can do everything?

Answer: This is not the best way to understand the issue. It is man who has the power to do. He then projects this power multiplied many times on an image that he calls God in order to find security. God does not act and yet everything is done through Him. Religions have often corrupted your intelligence instead of leading you towards self-knowledge, teaching you introspection and silence and encouraging you to develop metaphysical inquiry. They have invented all kinds of sins that have bound you to a mental image in which you have become hopelessly lost. The result is that man, a little being, invents a Big Being who, according to His whims, will save, protect or punish him and will either guarantee his life in paradise or condemn him to eternal damnation. When will you grasp that this is merely a projection of a parental image reproducing a system of rewards and punishment, Heaven and Hell, which nourishes fear and guilt? You believe in God? Excellent, but sharpen your intelligence for it alone can save you. I keep advising you to read the mystics of the great traditions, to develop a religious culture and, above all, to question yourself. Just as the energy of: "I really want to know but am ignorant" will open wide the Gates of Heaven, the energy of "I know, I believe, I am sure" will close them. Be like a scientist. Advance by the light of what you can verify and, little by little, you will lose your conditioning. Your brain is possessed by your mental activity. It creates problems in order to solve them. If you really see this, your mind stops dead. And when it stops dead, you find what you call God. It is just life tasting itself in the total absence of conditioning.

It is the unity of life recognizing itself as such in you emptied of your ego. God, unity – life – has neither will nor power, nor does it divide into separate parts. Only in that state, free from fear, can man truly be good.

Question: You keep telling us that God wants nothing, yet I feel loved by Him.

Answer: You have developed a love for yourself by using God. That is excellent for when you say that God loves you, you are saying that a part of you loves you. That part is already above the shadow. You have engaged on the path of love known in India as bhakti. On this path, the part of you where you love yourself will grow until it occupies the whole of you. God is the support of this growth. As long as you do not attach yourself to one of His representatives by putting up a photo in a shrine at home or by spreading rose petals at the Blessed One's feet, it may work. But you also need to ask why the planet is in the state it is in if God really loves us? Our identity is a personal consciousness. The substance of that consciousness is thought.

To deal with fear, man has created the concept of a personal God, the concept of a Saviour. You project an identity which you call God but it is a very limited concept in the way you use it. Is it not sad to reduce the energy of life that created the galaxies, the whole cosmos, to a concept that is no more than a wish to be protected by a Big Daddy? The energy of life loves you unconditionally which is why you are here. This energy cannot love you conditionally the way someone would love you. You should instead ask yourself if consciousness identified with thought can be erased by a real question. Ask yourself if there is such a thing as consciousness free from thought, free from identification, free from God. And ask yourself if such a consciousness would not be one with the nature of love?

Question: What is my true nature?

Answer: It cannot be turned into an object. It is neither being nor non–being. It is beyond absence. It is where you are not. As soon as you are no longer there, your true nature appears and you realise that you have always been there. It is the conscious energy of life. It is pure love and as it has never been born, it can never die.

Question: You place considerable emphasis on dreams. Why are they so important?

Answer: There is at the heart of you an extraordinary intelligence that loves you and that keeps sending you every night without fail and without getting tired the same messages: what stage you are at, what you should do to raise your level of consciousness and on what particular aspect of yourself you should be working. But you hardly ever listen to this intelligence and most of the time do not even understand it. Yet its message is clear for it speaks in a symbolic language that belongs both to your personal and to the collective symbolic language. Learn the language of your dreams and you will see how you will speed up your evolution by using it.

You will discover that you have several types of dreams. One of these describes in one or two scenes the particular blockage that you now face. Another set ups a sequence of scenes depicting your psychological state. A first sequence will show your current issues, a second will point towards their causes and a third will offer a solution.

You will see that a part of you knows exactly the situation you are in. This inner intelligence will keep dealing with the same issue as long as it has not been relatively solved. That is the reason why you have recurring dreams. The same message is presented in different ways in order to open new neural connections. By going deeper into this new message, you have the opportunity to dig into your old repressed structures and to let go of them. Learn to listen to your inner intelligence and remember that dreams show you your issues, but do not solve them.

Question: I never remember my dreams in the morning. What should I do about it?

Answer: First, put a notebook by your bedside to write your dreams down. Then before falling asleep, tell yourself that you will remember them when you wake up. As you wake up, do not move, slip about two thirds of the way back into sleep and, after a few moments, the images will rise to the surface. Go over the images several times so as not to forget them and, eventually, to catch a few more. When the images are firmly anchored, note down the dream and interpret it. You can also remember your dreams if you wake in the middle of the night or trigger their memory as you start your day through a thought association.

Question: And how do you do that?

Answer: The keys to your dream life are in a symbolic language that belongs only to you. As with any new language, you have to want to learn it. Its basic structure is in the various characters that feature in the dream.

To understand them is quite simple. Ask yourself: what does this specific character in his or her human quality symbolize for me today? What characteristics does he or she embody for me now? Once you have put these questions to yourself, you have to act fast and with determination to reach a correct answer. For the part of you that is about to be flushed out knows what you are up to and is going to try to confuse you with decoys, such as getting you to think about the interpretation later or coming up with a completely erroneous answer. That is why the question has to be whipped into action straightaway just like a horse before a jump.

To illustrate this, I will relate to you a dream that George, one of my students, had. In this dream he was walking along a New York street lined with brownstones and bathed in bright sunshine. He suddenly caught sight of a friend, Dr Walter. As he did not want to greet him, he crossed over to the other side of the street.

George asked me what his dream meant. To begin with, I questioned him about New York. His response was that for him the city was a symbol of freedom for it was there that at the age of nineteen he discovered what adult life was like. As bright sunshine symbolises consciousness, the theme of the dream was his journey towards consciousness and freedom.

What about his friend, Dr Walter? What characteristics, what human qualities did he symbolise?

The fact was that on three separate occasions – twice with girlfriends and once with his mother – the doctor had made a totally wrong diagnosis. George had also noted that Dr Walter treated his wife in a cold and contemptuous manner. He quickly realised the symbolic meaning of the doctor's character: he was a misogynist.

I explained to George that, in the case of his dream, it was not Dr Walter who was misogynistic but a group of sub-personalities representing an aspect of George's character. I then asked him to reduce the interpretation to one key phrase. He replied: "My misogynistic side is blocking my conscious path to freedom." Be aware that these aspects will always protect themselves as the individual's self-image would be threatened were it confronted by its reality.

Remember that one of the ego's key programs is to move towards the pleasant and to avoid the unpleasant. Faced by a repressed aspect that a part of you does not want to see, you are going to send yourself lures such as erasing the dream, not writing it down, putting off interpreting it until later, failing to interrogate it as sharply as you could or, while processing the dream, forgetting its key points. You will develop elaborate avoidance tactics so as not to confront the message that puts the equilibrium of your shadow at risk. When you interpret a dream, it is essential to maintain a good level of Distancing and to allow the energy released by the answers to filter through the whole of the body. A layer of your ego's armour, a wall of your fortress, will then be partially dismantled. The interpretation will bring up a new and precise message that will allow the drilling of Discernment to dig deeper into your layers. The only way to change is to see yourself as you really are and to be profoundly shaken by it. Interpreting your dreams will allow you to encounter this shock and will sharpen Discernment. This will help the dark energy that you have blocked and repressed to fragment. Remember too that this shock should only last a brief moment.

You need to learn the personal symbolic language of your dreams. While there is also a collective symbolism – water and the moon refer to the unconscious, the sun to the conscious mind and so on and so forth – you are dealing principally with your own symbolic language.

Let's say you dream of a car. Who is at the wheel? A friend. What are this friend's characteristics for you today? What do they symbolize? His presence in the dream means that the characteristics common to you both are in the driving seat of your life. If you dream of somebody, or of a group of people, that you do not know, this concerns an aspect of yourself of which you are not conscious as yet. To become acquainted with your own symbolic language is fascinating work. The more you gain mastery over it, the more enriched it will become. You will also discover that its messages are clear, coherent and precise and that they often show what you do not want to see in yourself.

The dream will frequently say the same thing twice to ensure that it is understood. Soon you will recognize the extraordinary willpower that this dream intelligence possesses and directs towards the development of your consciousness.

To interpret your dreams relatively well will take six months as long as you work at it regularly. To become good you will need a year. It is also very easy to get it wrong. It is vital to remember that while the intellect provides an answer, it is a physical sensation that comes from the movement of your shadow, of your old emotional body put at risk by the interpretation, that validates it.

Question: How do you avoid getting the interpretation wrong?

Answer: You must interpret your dream rigorously and be firm when asking: "What does this symbolize for me today?" Success lies in getting a rapid and spontaneous answer and in interpreting the information that you have gathered quickly. When you dream of a particular individual, you must apply the golden rule and ask: "What does this person's characteristics or human quality mean for me?" With experience, you will see that the reason that you shy away from interpreting is because there is something important in the dream that you do not want to see. Never forget that the ego is a defence system on permanent watch. The greater the risk to it, the cruder will be the methods by which it attempts to protect itself mechanically. The subtle and non-mechanical intelligence that you are creating through Distancing will realize this. Your intellect will often trick you into making poor interpretations, or will prevent you from pushing them as far as you can. It is essential to recognize the physical sensation that surges up once you have put your finger on the correct interpretation. This sensation, which is often accompanied by an emotional disturbance, confirms that you have hit the right symbolic key. The ability to recognize the vibration of the old emotional body, of the shadow, put at risk by interpretation, lies at the center of the decoding of the dream structure. Interpreting the dream is a morning exam that will show you the quality of your Distancing and of your Discernment. When you start your interpretation, you must first get the theme of your dream: for instance, the balance of your masculine and feminine side, that very special part that blocks you now, your relationship to business, the development of your soul.

Every dream has a theme. It is generally contained within the first image and is confirmed thereafter. If you get the theme, your chances of falling for a wrong interpretation diminishes.

To become good at this exercise, you need to develop two qualities, two new subpersonalities: a detective and an interpreter. First, the detective collects the evidence. He will ask a set of questions and demand rapid answers. Little by little the message of the dream will appear like the slow emergence of a Polaroid picture. The detective will refrain from coming to any conclusions before the end of the investigation. Once all the information has been gathered together, the interpreter will transform it into one or two short and sharp phrases that you will write down in your dream book. When making an effort to remember these phrases, you will see your old logic that will try to make you forget them. As you become aware of this, you will strengthen your directional ego. Your Discernment will be better able to cross the defences of the layers that you are trying to dismantle.

The more you interpret your dreams, the more you will see that you are designed to evolve, that life loves you unconditionally and that it wants to help you dismantle your armour.

Question: Apart from interpretation, what else can I do with my dreams?

Answer: You can reprogram yourself by modifying dream images. It is a simple, logical process and works very well.

Question: How do I do that?

Answer: You need to consciously reprogram a part of yourself. As soon as you have verified the truth of the statement I made earlier, namely that the dream intelligence sends you clear, coherent and precise messages, you can move on to the next stage, which is to respond to your unconscious in its own language. You must then, like a scientist, be the objective witness of this experiment.

Let us return to the example of Dr Walter, who for my student, George, represented an aspect of himself whose relationship towards women was twisted. You recall that the basic elements of the dream were a sunny street in New York, George avoiding Dr Walter by crossing the road etc. What George must do next is to search in his memory for a friend who is the direct opposite of this misogynistic personality: in other words, someone who is enormously fond of women. Once George has identified this individual, keeping the same background details, he replaces the image of Dr Walter with that of his women-loving friend. Instead of crossing the road to avoid him, he imagines himself walking up to him and warmly shaking his hand. He visualizes this image just before falling asleep in a very relaxed state of mind.

Remember that the dream is a message destined for your consciousness and that it communicates using the symbolic language of your unconscious. If you reprogram the unconscious through the modification of the images of the dream, it will accelerate the dismantling of your shadow.

The technique requires attentiveness and perseverance. You will sometimes feel your emotional body reacting within your physical body when you reprogram yourself. This can be quite unpleasant as the emotional body, the shadow, will use physical or mental decoys to resist change. In spite of that, it is fascinating work which needs to be practiced regularly. Do it well and you will soon see your attitude to the external world begin to modify.

* See Glossary

SEX, MONEY, WAR AND PEACE

Question: How can I control my sexual energy?

Answer: Before attempting to control it, you should first let it express itself. Between consenting adults there need be no barriers. As long as this is firmly established at the heart of your directional ego, your guilt will be less active. Sexuality is an energy that serves your pleasure, helps you build your relationships and opens onto family life. No longer enslaved by what is repressed, you will find a balance that will allow you to select between your real needs increasingly free from thoughts and fantasies, and your false needs triggered by the same old mental mechanisms, the same old connections to your shadow.

Question: I've heard that retaining my semen will help my spiritual growth.

Answer: Have you not read the recent British medical study that suggests that the practice of masturbation from an early age diminishes the risks of prostate cancer by 30 to 40 percent?

Question: But religions tell us the exact opposite.

Answer: Fortunately for us all, science and modern research are gradually lessening the power of the old religious systems, even though the latter still fight tooth and nail to hold on to their dominion. When apparently revealed pseudo-divine rules crumble, the global reach of guilt diminishes and the general level of consciousness increases.

Just as man was not created 5,000 years ago from nothing over seven days, and just as the sun does not revolve around the earth, so masturbation is not a sin but is even beneficial to health.

What does someone keen on power want? More power, of course. Religious systems, like most human organisations, are led by people who are often religious in name only and whose primary goal is to hold onto or to increase their power base. These men of power will fight for the system that they have identified with by trying to control others through fear and guilt. It is the raising of consciousness, improved education and the yearning for self-knowedge that will liberate humanity from its archaic belief systems.

Question: How should we live our sexuality?

Answer: By allowing your desires to express themselves freely. Sexual energy is the motor of the species onto which you should not impose your guilt, your fears, your anxieties. Then, quite naturally, it will leave the shadows and turn into something beautiful. Have you seen those Hindu statues in which gods and goddesses embrace in an union motivated by no more than the taste for pleasure? Why not take a leaf out of their book?

Question: That sounds a wonderful idea, but how do I go about it?

Answer: Start by accepting all your sexual desires and you will see how guilt, through thought, uses them in order to reinforce itself. Do remember that systems of thought are our main grabbing points. You cannot be free unless you lose them in one go.

Try to live your sexuality without images, without fantasising, without thought. Like scientists, observe what happens, staying within the world of sensation and interfering as little as possible with what you find. A sexuality accompanied by fantasies and images is masturbatory. It is not making love. In an evolutionary sexuality, the images will gradually disappear and will be replaced by emotions of increasing purity.

Question: Why do sex and money condition our lives to such an extent?

Answer: For most people money means power. Look at those natural history documentaries that describe the social relations that exist in monkey, baboon, chimpanzee and great ape colonies. The individual struggles to be an alpha male or female, or to be as close as possible to one of them. We function in exactly the same manner. In all societies the individual seeks the best status that he can achieve in the hierarchy. He wants wealth, or to be on best terms with whoever is the richest member of the tribe. He wants to give orders, or to have the ear of whoever has the most power. We all want to be near the top of the hierarchy. The reason why mystics have often put poverty to the fore is to help the individual to let go of his grabbing points. That is why in the Beatitudes Jesus said: "Blessed are the poor in spirit for theirs is the Kingdom of Heaven". Poor in spirit means to have surrendered all identifications.

The more money one has, the more power one has. Its loss or the fear of its loss will trigger fear or anxiety. Sex and seduction provide the most easily accessible compensatory systems to permit us not to face up to what we do not want to confront. They are grabbing points that can become major addictions. Sex is the driving force of our species onto which we have imposed repressed structures that have nothing to do with it. So, for instance, while meditating or reading a text, sexual thoughts will seize hold of us. We must let them drift by and ask: "Why are they emerging? What logic pushes them forward?"

We should look at our thoughts linked to sex and money. As soon as we recognise them as crutches, we should throw them away. We need to understand when they turn into compensatory behaviour. Let us carefully examine these aspects of ourselves. We will acknowledge how they are often manipulated by the fears and guilt that we carry within our shadow. As we dismantle them, we raise our level of consciousness and see that sex and money are just neutral energies which help us to find happiness. In so doing, we open ourselves more to joy which, little by little, becomes our nature. Let us try to be aware when we lose it. Once we have learnt to live in a joyful relationship with sex and money, they will no longer condition our lives in the same old way and we will be more successful.

Question: I am a businessman. How do I strike the right balance between what you are saying and my work?

Answer: Your ambition to succeed financially walks hand in hand with your desire to raise your level of consciousness. That is good. Remember that the nature of the ego is to want to grow indefinitely. It wants to grow financially just as it wants to grow spiritually. To ensure your true growth, you need to understand your own mechanisms. Make sure that you keep to an eighty/twenty split. Eighty percent for business, for all the battles in which you must engage, as well as for your love life; and, most importantly, twenty per cent for your spiritual life. In the eighty per cent, you will remain a conscious and ethical warrior, as well as a kind partner. But in the remaining twenty per cent you will be a seeker, practicing introspection, meditating and reading the mystics.

Question: How am I going to succeed in business then?

Answer: By having a well-built directional ego that masters your fears and your guilt. The more you dominate them, the more consciously and ethically you will behave in your various battles. The warrior who fights your battles in business must remain above the shadow in order to avoid losing choices. For that to happen, he must submit to the seeker in you. It is this seeker that will build the new tools of your success.

Once you have identified and drilled enough times the unconscious mass of your losing choices, your shadow will begin to lose its power. Its influence on your speech and actions will no longer be the same. You will see that you react and overcompensate less. Remember that the first layers are the most difficult to clear. Thereafter everything becomes much easier.

Discernment has opened a new conscious space within your unfurling thought processes. A new winning conscious ego begins to take shape. Little by little, you recognize the losing thoughts that come from your shadow because you spot the density of energy that they convey. Winning thoughts are linked to a tingly and lighter density of energy that filters through the head, the arms, the abdomen, then progressively through the whole body.

After a while these energetic frequencies will increase in intensity. Remain conscious of these sensations. Learn to recapture them whenever you lose them. That is how you will ride your shadow and remain where the conscious winning choices are for you will have learnt to recognise them not through your intellect but through sensation.

Question: So, where do I start from?

Answer: Settle on an objective and never let it go. Although you do not know how you will get there, don't entertain doubts. You also need to develop three qualities. Firstly, intuition which you must learn to recognise and to which you must listen as this will take you in the right direction. Secondly, magnetic power for it is with a powerful charisma that you will open doors and sell your products, your advice, your skills. The more you dismantle your fears, your shyness, your low self-esteem, the more your magnetic power will be effective. The final quality you need is the ability to see the material and psychological reality that surrounds you as it is, and not as you project it to be. As long as your vision of reality matches what is, you will move from one winning choice to another. Unfortunately your repressed fears and guilt can create a veil of anxiety and of greed that colour the situation. The results will be irrational levels of optimism or of pessimism. It is because of them that you disconnect from reality and keep making losing choices.

Once you have attained success, remain alert. Never cease to sharpen your mind to keep the seeker in you growing. Understand that success has put the logic of the choice of least harm* at risk. You are now above your shadow but success has disturbed your inner guilt balances which may provoke you to make unconscious losing choices.

Napoleon was broadly successful until 1812 when he made the losing choice of invading Russia. Richard Nixon, after his re-election, sewed the seeds of disaster by recording his conversations in the White House and lying about them. To manage success implies a high level of vigilance. In his bid to supersede Rupert Murdoch, Robert Maxwell overextended himself and defrauded his employees' pension funds to prop up his share price. Richard Fuld, the CEO of Lehman Brothers, increased the firm's risk to subprime mortgages even after the market had exposed the weakness of that sector, and missed the opportunity to sell a quarter of the shares which would have saved the company. There are many examples of people who reach a certain level of success and who then sabotage themselves. Think of political leaders who destroy their career through sex scandals. What will ensure lasting success is the constant maintenance of your Distancing and the growth of your inner seeker. The sign of a truly evolved being is that he can control himself without effort.

Question: Why do we have to fight to survive?

Answer: Ask yourself from where the notion that you have to fight to survive comes?

Question: But hasn't man always had to fight to survive?

Answer: As man's mind is creative, to uphold this system of belief is to make it into a reality. It is true that we humans are a violent and combative species. If you have any doubts, look at our history. But when you work on yourself, you bring your consciousness to a level where you can live above your energies of fear and of violence. It is at that level that you can change everything.

Question: Is world peace an attainable goal?

Answer: The twentieth century was an unending series of conflicts. The First World War caused ten million fatalities, the Second World War sixty. Since 1945, the development of arms has become more sophisticated and expensive. The cost of a B2 bomber, for instance, exceeds the military budget of most of the world's nations.

In the farewell speech that President Eisenhower gave on January 17th 1961, he warned us to keep the power of the military-industrial complex in check. The problem is not so much whether world peace is attainable as the mind-set of those who govern the world.

Wars since time immemorial have been triggered by men determined to extend or maintain their power base. As long as fear generates a yearning for power, this will inevitably have tragic consequences. Peace can only prevail if those who govern us are guided by wisdom. Unfortunately wise rulers, such as the Roman philosopher and Emperor Marcus Aurelius, are the exception.

The Founding Fathers of the United States, as well as their first Presidents, shared the values of the Enlightenment. They had a humanistic culture and aspired to a certain degree to wisdom. It is this ideal that needs to be sought. The critical question is how a brilliant and power-hungry ego, such as a ruler's, can change and seek to know himself.

An intelligent mind, dogged by a powerful shadow, will go much faster in the knowledge of himself than someone who is weak-willed and not that bright. In the Book of Revelation, John the Divine writes that God said: "... because you are lukewarm, and neither cold nor hot, I will spew you out of my mouth." There is no such thing as equality in the manifest, only competition; yet the goal of life is not power, but freedom and awakening.

If this idea enters, however slightly, the minds of the powerful, they will change at some level and, if they change, everything can change. We desperately need rulers who aspire to the light.

PART III
BIOGRAPHIES AND SELECTED TEXTS

INTRODUCTION

This chapter, which constitutes a small anthology of non-dualistic philosophy, has been put together to help readers reach three goals.

The first goal is for readers to understand that the path that leads to freedom has been taught by the awakened teachers of all major traditions, and that the time they spend studying this philosophy will bring them closer to their real nature.

The second goal is to encourage readers to develop a taste for challenging themselves with the right questions so that they can experience the very special pleasure of feeling their psychological structure shaken midsentence.

The third goal is for readers to understand that only sharp metaphysical thoughts can free them from the systems of belief that form them.

The nature of belief systems is to seek continuity. If a monk locks himself up for several years in a cell, concentrates on the wounds of his Lord Jesus Christ and identifies with his sufferings, he may manifest stigmatas, as have many Christian mystics. This is not a miracle for there is no such thing as a miracle. Remember: nature does not break its own rules. These wounds will have been created by a fusion between the conscious and the collective unconscious, an amazing and powerful force. But as life and evolution generally function well, this force only arises when man has lost his ego, and thus his desire.

Today quantum physics, the physics of possibility, provides us with rational explanations for these phenomena, arguing that we do not see an objective reality but a reality conditioned by the observer.

Man's thought, which is creative, has come up with theological constructs that have turned into powerful society-structuring archetypes. For these systems to last, their anchor points must be strong. This explains why hope-based, guilt-compensating concepts such as the Return of Christ Triumphant, the Mahdi, the Final Judgment, the Hidden Imam, the Messiah and the End of Time lie at the heart of all monotheistic religions. As everything in the eternal present is pre-existent, we should be careful about our beliefs.

Take the example of Revelations, Chapter 13, verses 16–17. "And he cause all, both small and great, rich and poor, free and bond, to receive a mark in their right hand, or in their foreheads. And that no man might buy or sell save he that had the mark or the name of the Beast or the number of his name."

This passage was written some 2,000 years ago, yet it is only now in the developed nations that such a level of technology is feasible. To buy a newspaper, for example, an individual would place his hand over an electronic eye that would debit his account. Before this vision of the future, we could respond with anxiety, a reaction that the ego is sure to encourage as it is one of its main grabbing points.

Requiring grabbing points, the mind generates all manner of fantasies, some of which then come true. We have created our own environment. Much of what we see around us has come into existence through thought. If we want life to continue on this planet, we must stop feeding the massive amounts of fear and guilt that promote the worst and often bring it about. Let us instead harness thought into serving self-knowledge. Let us listen to the awakened teachers of the perennial philosophy who transcend religions and are to be found in all traditions. They express what unifies the human race and show us how we can develop ourselves and integrate our real nature.

ANGELUS SILESIUS

1624–1677. Angelus Silesius was born in a prosperous Lutheran family in Silesia. He studied medicine, converted to Catholicism and lived for three years in silence. His work is in the lineage of Meister Eckhart, Tauler and Böhme. For him, man is nothing before his Creator and yet it is only through man that God can find completion. Man must therefore empty himself of himself to become what he truly is.

"I am not outside God and God is not outside me."

"God is an utter nothingness
Beyond the touch of Time and Space.
The more thou graspest after Him,
The more he fleeth thy embrace."

"Be still, Beloved. Be still. If you become pure silence, God will give you more than you have ever wished for."

"I know that without me God cannot live for an instant; if I come to nothing. then He must give up his being."

"The beast will become man and man will become angelic and the angel God when you are fully healed."

Just like Rumi and Hinduism, Angelius Silesius speaks to us of our potential evolution.

ASHTAVAKRA GITA

The Ashtavakra Gita expresses the teachings of the Upanishad and of Advaita Vedanta. It does not express truth through rational discourse but describes the state of an enlightened being. Each verse is a meditative text. It is by assimilating its verses that the student, if he is ready, opens himself to truth.

"You are changeless, independent, calm, without dimension or form, unshakeable. Your nature is an intelligence beyond measure. Understand that you are pure consciousness."

"Everything which came out of me is resolved back into me like a pot back into soil, a wave into water, and a bracelet into gold."

"The idea of duality is the root of all suffering. The only remedy is the perception of the unreality of all objects and the realization of one's self as unity, pure intelligence and bliss."

"You are not the body, nor is the body yours. You are not the doer of actions nor the reaper of their consequences. You are eternally pure consciousness, the witness, in need of nothing – so live in joy."

"You are pure consciousness, and the world is not separate from you. So the idea of accepting or rejecting whatever is meaningless."

AVADHUT GITA

The Avadhut Gita is a classical text designed for students who have already made considerable progress in the study of metaphysics. Just like the Astavakra Gita, its origin lies in the Upanishads that, along with Advaita Vedanta, form the heart of Hinduism. It addresses those whose life goal is to realize the ultimate truth and to be eternally free.

"The subtle faculties of touch, taste, smell, form and sound which constitute the world without are not yourself, nor are they within you. You are the great all-transcending Reality." Chapter 1, Verse 16.

"Know all forms, physical and subtle, as illusion. The Reality underlying them is eternal. By living this Truth one passes beyond birth and death." Chapter 1, Verse 21.

"There are some that prize non-dualism, others hold to dualism. They know not the Truth, which is above both." Chapter 1, Verse 34.

"I am the eternal principle. Free from attachment and aversion, free from imperfections am I. Fate and providence exist not in me. Eternally free from the sufferings of the world, verily, space-like immortality-giving Knowledge am I." Chapter 1, Verse 31.

BHAGAVAD GITA

The Bhagavad Gita, a spiritual guidebook drawn from the Mahabharata, tells of the conflict between two clans. Through the teachings of Krishna, Arjuna, the leader of one of the clans, is brought from the human level to the divine via the paths of action or karma, love or bhakti, and knowledge or gnana. Along with the Upanishads, the Gita is one of the sources of Hinduism. Many of the great Indian philosophers have written commentaries on the Gita.

"He who sees me in all things and sees all things in me, I do not separate from him and he does not separate from me."

"Enveloped in the illusion that I generate, I am not known by all. The blind world does not know me, I, the unborn, the indestructible."

"Oh, Arjuna, four types of people adore me. Those who suffer, those who seek knowledge, those who seek personal salvation, and the wise. The wise who lives in constant harmony, who loves the One, is the most perfect. In truth I am supremely dear to the wise and he to me."

JACOB BÖHME

1575–1624. He worked as a village cobbler until he awakened spiritually at the age of 25 and wrote down his experiences even though forbidden to do so by the church authorities. He belongs to the same tradition as Meister Eckhart and the Rhenish mystics.

"All reflection upon and study of the Will of God is in vain unless accompanied by a transformation of the spirit."

"But how may I seize it without the death of the will?"

"If you want to seize it, it runs away from you. But if you surrender entirely to it, then you die to yourself according to your own will and it becomes the life of your own nature. It does not make you die but on the contrary brings you alive according to its own life. You thereafter live not according to your will but according to its Will, for your will becomes its Will. And so you die to yourself but live in God."

"The ego, in its most compact form, is the very root of all evil."

For further reading: Jacob Böhme. The Three Principles of the Divine Essence.

BUDDHISM
Founded by Shakyamuni, born in 563 BC, as a response to suffering. The origin of suffering is belief in the ego, whose ruling principle is to perpetuate our individuality through desire. This itself stems from ignorance. You run one desire after another. The illusion of duration comes from a mental trick caused by attachment. Through introspection and meditation arise a profound understanding that ends in awakening.

Words of the Buddha:

"You are your own refuge. There is none other. This refuge is difficult to build. The I is our master. There is none other. This master is difficult to liberate. You cannot save another. You can only save yourself. If you commit a bad act, you will reap bitter fruit. If you do not commit it, your I will be purified."

"The extinction of desire, the extinction of anger, the extinction of illusion, that is what is called Nirvana."

"Hatred does not end hatred. Hatred only ends with love."

"The purpose of life is not to acquire a reputation, nor to become morally impeccable, nor to focus on scholarship. It is the unshakeable deliverance of the heart. That is the goal of a holy life. That is its essence and its end."

CH'AN OR ZEN
Introduced in China from India by Bodhidharma (470–543 AD), this school is today known in Japan as Zen. Its key principles are: a special transmission from mind to mind; no dependence on words and texts; teachings to be directed at man's heart, as therein lies the nature of Buddha. This will only be integrated once you understand that you have no reality whatsoever as a divided being. This sudden realization is awakening.

DEEPAK CHOPRA

Born 1946. Indian doctor and philosopher who has provided a new understanding of Hinduism to millions and has helped to raise the level of awareness in the United States by offering access to a spiritual culture several thousand years old.

"Pure consciousness is always present in everything, no matter what world it occupies or form it takes."

"The physical has the least amount of pure consciousness because it is dominated by physical things and the illusion of separatedness."

"The invisible world comes first. It contains the seeds of time and space."

"Belief allows you to gain access to certain experiences but blocks you from others."

"Sometimes the enemy is outside but if you look carefully you will see that he is always within."

"Reality increases the closer you get to the source."

For further reading: Deepak Chopra. Life After Death: The Book of Answers.

DALAI LAMA

Born in 1935, Tenzin Gyatso is the 14th Dalai Lama and is recognized as the spiritual head of Tibetan Buddhism. For Tibetans he is the incarnation of the Buddha of Compassion.

"The worst aspect of pride is that it prevents us from improving."

"If we are not kind towards ourselves, we cannot be kind towards others. And if we do not work to change our attitude, we have little chance of finding peace and joy."

"The more we learn about the void and the interdependence of all things, the more it is difficult to accept at the same time the idea of a Creator existing by Himself and immutable."

"To follow the one through whom we will see our faults, and through whom we will increase our qualities just like the waxing moon, to hold as more precious than life itself this Supreme Guardian is the practice of a boddhisattva."

"He who teaches should speak only of what he has experienced."

"To have an intellectual understanding of the meaning of the void is not the same as having a realization of the void."

"All the Buddhas like Shakyamuni who became awakened were at one time just like us and at the same level of consciousness as us."

For further reading: Dalai Lama. The Art of Happiness: A Handbook for Living by His Holiness.

ALBERT EINSTEIN
Born 1879, died 1955, the physicist Albert Einstein encompassed the fundamental unity of all things by linking matter and energy within one law.

"A man's true worth is determined by examining the extent to which he has managed to liberate himself from his ego."

"Man experiences the nullity of human wishes and will and discovers perfection at the point where the world of nature corresponds to the world of thought. At that moment Being understands that its individual existence is a kind of prison and yearns to embrace the totality of the Manifest that strikes him as a perfectly intelligible entity."

"According to the general theory of relativity, the concept of space dissociated from all physical contents does not exist."

"We envisage matter as something which can neither be created nor destroyed."

"Even if the worlds of religion and of science are clearly separated, there nonetheless exist between them strong relations of reciprocity and of interdependence. The situation can be illustrated in the following manner: science without religion is hobbled, and religion without science is blind."

For further reading: Albert Einstein. The World as I See it.

GURDJIEFF
1877–1949. Gurdjieff, a spiritual Master, considered that man exists in a state of hypnosis or sleep and that he is a machine moved by a series of mechanical functions.

"One of the best ways of awakening the desire to work on oneself is to realize that one may die at any moment, and this is something that you must learn not to forget."

"All the prophets sent from Above have spoken of the death which could manifest in this life, that is to say the death of the 'tyrant' from which the slavery which affects us in this life stems, a death on which man's first and principal freedom depends."

"The first requirement, the first condition, the first test for whoever wishes to work on himself is to change his appreciation of himself. Not only must he imagine, think and believe, he must also see certain things in himself which he had not seen before, and see them for real. His appreciation will never change if he continues to see nothing in himself. And to see, he must learn to see. That is man's first initiation into self-knowledge."

"It is very important for the man who works on himself to realize that change can only occur if he changes his attitude to the external world."

"Conscious love evokes the same response.
Emotional love provokes its opposite.
Physical love depends on type and polarity."

For further reading: In Search of the Miraculous, Fragments of an Unknown Teaching. P.D. Ouspenski.

HADEWIJCH OF ANTWERP

1220–1260. Hadjwich was a Beguine, a member of a religious community living under rules less strict than a convent. Her writings deal with mystical union and were produced for the members of her order. They became known long after her death.

"Do not allow your thoughts to wander here and there, but let them find their joy only in eternity."

"Whatever your senses perceive, keep your inner realm in eternity, however painful it may be for you to feel yourself fought over by two beings."

"The circle of things must be restricted and annulled so that the circle of nakedness, once grown and expanded, embraces the infinite."

"In the bosom of the One, souls are pure and internally naked, without images or shapes, as if freed from time uncreated and unrestricted by limits."

"Everything is confined: I feel so vast. What I have wished to seek eternally is an uncreated reality."

"The soul, established in pure nakedness, in pure mortality, gives rise to everything that is and that will be."

For further reading: Hadewijch. The Complete Works.

HALLÂJ

857–922. A Sufi mystic, Hallaj experienced a union of burning love within which life itself is consumed. For him, the purpose of life is to unify with God. Human personality must destroy itself in order to be invaded by Him. He was accused of blasphemy for having said: "I am the truth, my I is God." For this statement he was crucified in Baghdad on the 26th March, 922.

"When God takes hold of a heart, he empties it of what is not Him."

"Know that man who proclaims the unity of God affirms himself."

"I have meditated on the many religions in order to understand them and have found that they give rise to a single principle with numerous ramifications. Do not ask an individual to adopt a particular religion for this would separate him from the fundamental principle. It is this very principle which should search for him."

For further reading: The Kitab al Tawasin.

HSIN-HSIN MING

The Hsin Hsin Ming (lit. Trust Mind Inscription), is one of the earliest and most influential Ch'an texts. It was written by Chien-chih Seng-ts'an, the third Chinese patriarch, in the seventh century. It is regarded as the perfect expression of Ch'an Buddhist metaphysics.

"The Great Way is not difficult,
Just don't pick and choose.
If you cut off all likes or dislikes
Everything is clear like space.

Make the slightest distinction
And heaven and earth are set apart.
If you wish to see the truth,
Don't think for or against.

Likes and dislikes
Are the mind's disease.
Without understanding the deep meaning
You cannot still your thoughts.

It is clear like space,
Nothing missing, nothing extra.
If you want something
You cannot see things as they are.

Outside, don't get tangled in things.
Inside, don't get lost in emptiness.
Be still and become One
And all opposites disappear.

If you stop moving to become still,
This stillness always moves.

If you hold on to opposites,
How can you know One?"

HUANG PO

In the IXth century Huang Po, a Ch'an Master and the Master of Lin-Chi (see below), became one of the precursors of the Rinzai school, which still exists in Japan. His speeches and sermons are among the most profound of Ch'an Buddhism. He died in 850 AD.

"The ordinary person holds onto objects, the seeker holds onto Mind. But forgetting both objects and Mind is the true law. Forgetting objects is easy but forgetting the Mind is very hard. Man does not dare forget the Mind. He is afraid of falling into a void in which there will be nothing to hold onto. That is because he does not understand that the fundamental void is not void. But only in the law are things that way."

"Awakening has no place. No more did Buddha reach awakening than living beings lose it. It can neither be attained through the body nor sought with the spirit. Awakening is not something one finds. You need to produce the spirit of that which is unfindable and when you find absolutely nothing, that will be the spirit of awakening. Awakening is nowhere to be found, which is why nobody can find it."

"Error has no substance, being entirely the product of our thinking processes. Were you to prevent all conceptual movement of thought and to stop your mental processes, errors would naturally disappear for you."

"To realize that nothing exists in reality onto which one can actually fasten is the perfect and supreme wisdom."

"Everything comes down to the spirit, and yet this spirit is also unfindable. So what is one seeking?"

For further reading: Huang Po. The Zen Teachings of Huang Po on the Transmission of Mind.

HUI NENG

638–713. Sixth Patriarch of the Ch'an School. He teaches his students that all suffering comes from man's attachment to his ego and thus to the world. He is the founder of the School of Sudden Enlightenment. He insists that the method is beyond polarities and is neither sudden not progressive. For him: "Everything depends on the speed or the dullness of the spirit. The study of the doctrine of the School of Sudden Enlightenment cannot be brought to completion by dullards."

"Those beings who study the Great Path and who have the energy to observe themselves with attention belong to the same category as those beings who have a lucid intelligence."

"The great Masters who have transmitted the teaching of sudden illumination and those who have the will to study it make up a whole."

"The Teaching requires thousands of means but their many divergences converge towards unity. In the cavern of your obscure and secret passions, from an ordinary moment will be born the sun of generosity."

"If you really practice the path, you will see no faults in this world. To see subjects of criticism in this world testifies that you are yourself criticisable."

"The ego is responsible for the criticism of others. You are naturally guilty of the criticisms that come from the ego. It is only through the suppression of the spirit of criticism that the defilements, passions and useless gossiping will be completely destroyed. Wrong views belong to this world and the true view is the exit from it, but understand that both wrong and true views must disappear."

"In the very heart of me, there is a Buddha.
This inner Buddha is the true Buddha.
If you did not already have in you the spirit of Buddha,
Where would you seek it?"

For further reading: The Platform Sutra of Hui Neng.

IBN ARABÎ

1165–1240. A scholar, Ibn Arabi spent his life travelling and influenced the Islamic world through the three hundred books that he wrote. He asserted that to discover the truth, man must first come to know himself through his spiritual essence and can only know himself in and through God. Ibn Arabi's formulation is paradoxical. He prevents the reader's mind from becoming stuck and brings him to the point of surrender by unbalancing his rationality.

"The existence of created things is the very existence of the Creator."

"God is therefore the mirror in which you see yourself, just as you are the mirror in which he contemplates his names."

"If you think that God is transcendent, start to think that He is immanent. If you think that God is immanent, start to think that He is transcendent."

For further reading: The Mysteries of Bearing Witness to the Oneness of God and the Prophethood of Ibn-Al-Arabi.

JESUS

For Christians, Jesus is the only Son of God who came to earth and suffered death for man's sins. The ruling principle of his teaching is love. For Islam, he belongs to the lineage of prophets.

"Blessed are the poor in spirit for theirs is the Kingdom of Heaven."
Matthew 5.3.

"Verily I say unto you, whomsoever shall not receive the Kingdom of Heaven as a little child, he shall not enter therein."
Mark 10.15

"While our outer man is consumed, our inner man renews from day to day."
Corinthians 4.15.

"I and my Father are One." John 10.30.

The Gospel according to Thomas is a Gnostic text that was found near the Dead Sea in 1945. It stresses the non-dualistic aspects of Jesus' teaching, and above all the notion that salvation is an individual search. Many of its 113 sayings are similar to what is in the four Gospels.

Jesus said: "The kingdom of the Father is like a man who wanted to kill a powerful man. He unsheathed his sword in his house and pierced the wall to see whether he had a steady hand. Then he killed the powerful man."

Jesus said: "If you express that which is in you, what you express will save you. If you do not express that which is in you, what you do not express will destroy you."

Jesus said: "Split wood and you will find me there. Lift the stone and you will find me there."

Jesus said: "When you make the Two into One, you will become children of Adam, and when you say, 'Mountain, move from here!' it will move."

Jesus said: "How miserable is the body that depends on a body, and how miserable is the soul that depends on these two."

Jesus said: "Those who seek should not stop seeking until they find. When they find, they will be disturbed. When they are disturbed, they will marvel, and will reign over all. He who finds the interpretation of these words will not taste death."

For further reading: The Gospel according to Thomas.

CARL JUNG
1875-1961. A close collaborator of Freud who moved away from him to create his own doctrine, complex psychology. He formulated a number of new concepts: the collective unconscious, the archetypes, synchronicity. For him, man can only be fulfilled if he has an understanding of his unconscious life. His psychological approach is close to Hinduism and Buddhism. At the end of his life he searched for confirmation of his thesis in mystical writings.

"Nothing has been accomplished until the individual in his very being has been transformed."

"The reality of the soul is my working hypothesis. My main activity lies in assembling, describing and explaining facts which are non-manifest."

For further reading: C.G. Jung. Modern Man in Search of a Soul.

KABBALAH
The word Kabbalah means reception in Hebrew. The Kabbalah is a sacred, magical and metaphysical path through which the most profound understandings of Jewish mysticism are expressed. It defines a number of spheres and axes which realize the reception of light from the upper world via the intermediary into the lower in which we find ourselves. These axes and spheres are represented in the Tree of Life that links the upper, the middle and the lower worlds.

J. KRISHNAMURTI
1895–1986. Krishnamurti is a spiritual Master who rejected this role as well as all religions, viewing them as obstacles to knowledge. He considered that humanity, in spite of the advances of technology, has remained violent and barbaric and that evolution can only be achieved through individual work. He asked his audience to become seekers.

"In the whole world there are only two kinds of people: those who have knowledge and those who do not. Only knowledge matters."

"To understand the ego requires an enormous amount of intelligence, of vigilance and of skilful observation, a quality of observation which must be incessant so as not to weaken."

"Reality, truth, cannot be recognized. In order for truth to come about, it is vital that belief, experience, truth, the search for virtue – which is not the same thing as being virtuous – all of these disappear."

"To free the spirit of all its conditioning, one must have a total vision of it and this must operate in the absence of thought. That is not such a mystery. Try it out and see."

"Every gathering, be it of knowledge or of experience, all forms of ideals, all projections of the spirit, all deliberate practice aiming to reform the mind in the light of what it should be or should not be, all of these hobble our ability to investigate and discover."

For further reading: J. Krishnamurti. On Living and Dying.

KORAN
The Koran rules every aspect of a Muslim's life. It consists of six thousand and two hundred and twenty six verses, the surahs, which the faithful repeat infinitely.

"Surely Allah does not forgive that anything should be associated with Him, and forgives what is besides that to whomsoever He pleases; and whoever associates anything with Allah, he devises indeed a great sin. Koran 4.48."

"Say: He, Allah, is One.
Allah is He on Whom all depend.
He begets not, nor is He begotten.
And none is like Him."
Koran 112.

This fragment is fundamental. The Prophet, according to the tradition, is supposed to have said that it in itself was worth a third of the Koran.

LALLA DED
Born 1355, date of death unknown. Lalla Ded is said to have been born in Kashmir. Her poems convey the intensity of her mystical experience and of her spiritual metamorphosis. She recommends an ardent quest propelled by an intuitive awareness of unity and of divine love. She is considered by Muslims as a saint who converted to their religion.

"Knowing, be ignorant. Seeing, be blind. Listening, be deaf. Before all things be insensitive. Whatever people say to you, respond to what is. That is what you must really practise to know reality."

"He who considers others and himself as equal, he for whom day and night are the same and whose thoughts are free of duality, he and only he has seen the lord of the gods."

"I have seen the divine and its essential nature. Nothing exists, neither me, nor you, nor even the universe's unfurling."

"If you truly understand unity, you are no longer nowhere for by unity I was reduced to nothingness."

"When searching for the self, I tired myself out. For no one who has searched has ever found the secret science beyond thought. The moment I ceased to search, love guided me."

"There, concentrating, absorbed in a single thought, I took flight towards heaven and the path of the light."

For further reading: Lalla Ded. The Wise Sayings of Lal-Ded, A Mystic Poetess of Ancient Kashmir.

LAO TZU
570–490 BC. Lao Tzu is the author of the Tao Te Ching which means the Book of the Path and of Virtue. 'Tao' designates the original non-active principle. 'Te' is the spiritual and magical energy which it deploys. The Tao is in itself indescribable.

"The Tao is empty but boundless."

"The Tao does not act yet everything occurs through it."

"The Tao is the common source of all things."

"Supreme virtue ignores virtue which is why it is always virtuous. Secondary virtue cultivates virtue which is why it is not virtuous. Supreme virtue does not act and has no reason to act."

"Bathed in light from every side, one can be ignorant, give life, entertain it, produce without being acquisitive, act without counting the cost, direct without enslaving."

For further reading: Lao Tzu. Tao Te Ching.

LIEH TZU

Born 450 BC; date of death unknown. He is said to have lived on the generosity of his disciples. Along with Lao Tzu and Chang Tzu, he is one of the fathers of Taoism and his 'The Classic of Perfect Emptiness' is one of its founding texts.

"There is in him neither knowledge nor power and yet he is omniscient and omnipotent."

"Form is something that necessarily has an end and that is why heaven and earth will one day cease, and cease with us. Will that be the final end? We do not know. But there is to the Tao no end as its nature is to be without beginning. Nor are there extreme limits as the essence of the Tao is to be beyond all duration."

"Someone asked philosopher Lieh Tzu: "Why do you hold the void in such high esteem?" Lieh Tzu replied: "The void is not interested in esteem. If one wishes to be without a name, there is nothing quite like silence, quite like the void. It is through silence and the void that we return to our true home."

"The difference between inner and outer was blunted. There was no further difference between the sensations felt in eyes and ears, nose and mouth. All the senses fused into one. My spirit became fixed. My body was freed."

"Things are born from the formless and end where there is no longer any transformation for them. How could he who attains that state and understand it be fixed to things? By keeping himself in an attitude that is indifferent to all emotions, he seeks shelter in the infinite duration. He acts where things begin and end."

For further reading: Lieh Tzu. The Classic of Perfect Emptiness.

LIN-CHI

Lin-Chi, a Ch'an master and founder of the school which bears his name (Rinzai in Japan), and which over the centuries became the most important of the Ch'an schools, was known for his abrupt teaching practice. He died in 866 AD.

"It is because you have no confidence in yourself that you all rush after everything which is external to you, allowing yourself to be distracted by ten thousand objects and thus failing to attain independence. Learn to quieten this searching spirit which makes you run from thought to thought and you will be no longer different to a Buddha."

"Whoever understands the absence of grabbing points does not need to obtain Buddhahood."

"If you love sanctity while hating profanity, you will float and sink in the ocean of birth and death."

"It is when thought is born that the many things are born. When thought is destroyed, so are the many things."

For further reading: The Zen Teachings of Master Lin-Chi.

NISARGADATTA MAHARAJ

1897–1981. A modest shopkeeper who taught students in his house in Mumbai. His teachings were compiled in a bestselling book: 'I am That'. His lineage is Advaita Vedanta. One day he visits a Master who tells him: "You are not what you think you are. Find out what you are. Observe your sense of "I AM" and discover your real self." Maharaj commented: "And so I did what he told me to do. I dedicated my whole time to observing myself in silence. I required no more than three years to realize my true nature."

"Look at your thoughts as you would street traffic. People come and go. You record them but without reacting. It is not easy to begin with, but with practice you will notice that your mind can operate on several different levels at the same time, and that you can be conscious of them all. It is only when you focus on one particular level that your attention allows itself to be caught and that the other levels become dimmed. But even then these other levels continue to function, if out of the field of consciousness."

"You are only making one major error: you are mistaking the interior for the exterior and vice versa. You believe that what is in you is outside of you, and that what is outside of you is in you.

Mind and sensations are external, but you believe that they are intimately yours."

"You think that the world is objective when it is only a projection of your psyche. That is the fundamental mental confusion. You must really think of yourself externally. There is no other way."

"What is liberation after all? It is the knowledge that you are beyond birth and death. By forgetting who you are and imagining yourself a mortal creature, you create so much misery for yourself. You really must wake up from a bad dream."

"You are always searching for pleasure and attempting to avoid pain, always seeking peace and happiness. Can you not see that it is the search for happiness that is making you miserable?"

"Everyone is happy to be alive but few experience its full savour. You will manage to know it by remaining within the mind in the 'I am, I know, I love' with the desire to get to the bottom of those words."

"Desires are no more than waves in the mind. I do not feel motivated in any way to satisfy them nor do I feel like acting them out. To be free of one's desires means that the compulsion to satisfy them is absent."

For further reading: Nisargadatta Maharaj. I Am That.

MARCUS AURELIUS
121–181 AD. Roman emperor and Stoic philosopher during whose reign the empire prospered. The life of a Stoic philosopher requires a constant vigilance, profound observation, self-mastery, obedience to the laws of nature with the aim of reaching complete transfiguration and the expansion of the soul in joy.

"Do not behave as if you had thousand of years before you. Death approaches. While you are alive, as long as it is still in your power to do so, turn yourself into a man of righteousness."
Book 4, verse 17.

"Do not let the whirlpool drag you off. Between the various movements of your heart, choose what fits best with justice. And between your various imaginations, stay with what you have conceived clearly."
Book 4, verse 22.

"How easy it is to push back, to reduce to nil every imagination which does not fit or which disturbs the soul, and in an instant to recover complete serenity."
Book 5, verse 2.

"There is no such thing as evil for those who transform themselves, nor is there any good for those who survive at the end of this transformation."
Book 4 Verse 42.

"What is the point? What you must ask yourself on each and every occasion. And what you need to ask yourself is: what is the state of this part of me which is quite rightly called the guide? What soul do I now have? Is it the soul of a child, a young man, a feeble woman, a tyrant, a beast of burden, ferocious animal?"
Book 5, verse 1.

The concept of the subpersonalities and the practice of introspection are contained in this verse.

For further reading: Marcus Aurelius. Meditations.

MEISTER ECKHART

1260–1327. Meister Eckhart, a Dominican friar, was a Master of Rhenish mysticism. He died before the beginning of the trial which the Church intended him to stand. He insisted on the necessity of going outside one's self in order to penetrate eternity and to become One. Thus God's plan can be fulfilled.

"The higher a soul rises above itself and the more it is pure and clear, the more perfectly God can accomplish his Work through it according to its similarity to Him."

"Love in its highest and most pure level is nothing else but God."

"Empty your ego of yourself and of all things and consider what you are in God for that is the real you."

"When you reach the point where you no longer feel sorrow or anxiety about anything, and where sorrow is no longer sorrow for yourself, and where everything has turned into a deep peace for you, then you have truly been born."

"The soul must put its trust in God. God cannot bring about his divine Work in the soul when everything which enters it has become circumscribed by measures. A measure is what locks things from within and from without."

"What is the nature of God? To diffuse through Creation, to be the same at all times, to have, to want, to know nothing."

"Here man through his poverty has reconquered what he was eternally and will always be."

For further reading: Meister Eckhart. Treaties and Sermons.

NIFFARI
IXth-Xth century. A contemporary of Hallaj, Muhammad Ibn Al-Hasan An-Niffari's birthday varies. All records of him were lost for several centuries. The teaching contained in The Book of Standings exhorts the reader to be rid of all aspects in order to merge with unity.

"He said to me: 'I show myself to no eye, to no heart without destroying them."

Niffari also stresses the rise in consciousness through the tactile sensation that he calls the shimmering of the skin.

"He stopped me when I felt the shimmering of the skin and he said to me: 'It is one of the effects of my gaze, it is the door to my presence. He said to me: 'It is a fact of my authority and of no authority but mine. It is a fact of the authority of my coming towards you and not of the authority of you coming towards me. He said to me: 'It is a sign of my remembrance of you and not of your remembrance of me. It is my sign and my proof. Through it measure each passion and alliance. If it remains active, it is truth. If it does not remain active, it is a lie. He says to me: 'It is my scales. Rely on them. It is my compass. Gauge where you are by it. It is the sign of certainty and of accomplishment.'"

Above all Niffari's teaching is metaphysical.

"He says to me: 'If you see me, veiling and unveiling are the same. He says to me: 'Ignorance is the veiling of vision and knowledge is the veiling of vision. He who knows is in duality.'"

"He stopped me in the night and said to me: 'If the night comes to you, stop in my hands. Seize hold of ignorance. Chase from me knowledge of heaven and earth. If you do that, you will see me come down.'"

For further reading: The Book of Standings of Niffari.

RAMANA MAHARSHI
1879–1950. Ramana Maharshi awakened at the age of 17 while engaged in an introspection on death. He lived for many years as an ascetic in a cave. Later, drawn to his presence, disciples built him an ashram. His teachings are Advaita-Vedantan. He constantly brings the student back to the origin of the 'I' until through introspection this 'I' realizes its identity in the Self.

"The principle on which intellect is founded cannot be understood by the intellect."

"There is no greater mystery than this: we are reality and seek to obtain reality."

"Man thinks himself limited and therein lies the source of all his troubles."

"Facts are only real for those who see them. Pain and pleasure are not linked to facts but stem from mental concepts."

"You have externalised yourself which is why you have forgotten yourself. Dive deep into yourself and you will know that you are the Self."

"One must associate nothing with the pure Self."

"There is no creation, no destruction, no destiny, no choice, no way, no realization. This is the supreme truth."

For further reading: The Teachings of Ramana Maharshi.

ANANDAMAYI MAYI

1896–1982. When young, Anandamayi practised the ascetic life. From the age of thirty she taught a path in which love, joy and wisdom are inextricably linked. Although she defended Hindu doctrine, she attached herself to no dogma. She said: "Think of me as a Christian, a Hindu, a Muslim, or whatever you want."

"To find God means nothing more than finding your true self. To find all by losing all, that is what is truly desirable."

"Human beings must live in the cavern that is within them so that the Supreme Being that lives there can reveal himself."

"The human being is a traveler on the road to becoming a superman."

"This body keeps repeating the same thing to you over and over again. Be a pilgrim on the road to immortality. Flee from the path of death, travel towards immortality. Show that you cannot be destroyed, that you are immortal."

"In truth the Master is within you. You will realize nothing until you have discovered your inner Master."

"What you are searching for you will find if such is your thirst that it sharpens the fibre of your very being."

"You must adhere firmly, and without fail, to the practices destined to reveal the true nature of the individual and persevere in their exercise."

For further reading: The Teachings of Anandamayi Ma.

RABBI NACHMAN OF BRESLOV

1772–1810. Rabbi Nachman, the grandson of the Baal-Shem Tov, the Founder of Hassidism, gave a new impulse to Hasidic Judaism by combining the esoteric secrets of Kabbalah with the study of the Torah. He attracted thousands of disciples by offering a spiritual life and a practical solution to day-to-day problems.

"You are where your thoughts are. Ensure that your thoughts are where you wish to be."

"The highest form of peace is the one that harmonises opposites."

"The path of spiritual growth resembles a journey on a roller-coaster. Rest assured that progressively you will learn that the descending path is none but the preparation for the ascending."

"Devote yourself to good and the evil will fall away of its own accord."

"The light of the infinite has no form. It adopts the contours of whoever receives it."

For further reading: The Seven Beggars, the Empty Chair and other Stories.

PLATO

428–347 BC. A disciple of Socrates. In his allegory of the cavern, he explains how we can drop our illusory identifications and reconnect to the light of full consciousness. A number of prisoners are chained up in a cavern. A fire behind them projects their shadows onto its walls. Far behind this fire the light of day hardly reaches them. That world constitutes their reality. One of the prisoners manages to free himself from his chains and rejoins the full light of day.

"The wise man speaks because he has something to say, the fool because he wishes to say something."

"You must use pure thought to reach absolute truth."

"Reality is both multiple and unified and in its divisions it is always gathered together."

"Time is the ever moving image of eternity's stillness."

"The true mark of the philosopher is astonishment."

"True philosophers practice dying and they are among men the least afraid of dying."

For further reading: Plato. The Symposium.

PLOTINUS
205–270. Roman philosopher and mystic. Plotinus practices an experimental metaphysics. He teaches that there is a One that is totally transcendent beyond Being and non-Being. This One is the source of the universe. It contains no division, no multiplicity, no change. Plotinus establishes the analogy with the sun from which light emanates without in any way being diminished. The mystical aspect of his teachings appear when he speaks of enstasy rather than ecstasy to define the effects of his union with the One.

"It is through the One that all beings are beings."

"We must use the intellect as a guide to contemplate the One."

"To escape as one towards the One."

"Only vision, not teaching, can put you in contact with the One."

"Do not seek it as an object but as a presence."

"It is within that you must seek the universal presence of the One."

"Make the center of yourself coincide with the center of all things."

For further reading: The 9th Treatise of the 4th Ennead.

MARGUERITE PORETE
1250–1310. A member of a lay sisterhood, the Beguines, from northern France, Marguerite Porète's spiritual path is in the form of a teaching offered by Love to Reason. Her book 'A Mirror for Simple Souls' was forbidden and she was put on trial and burnt at the stake in Paris on the 1st of June 1310.

"This knowledge is so clear that it sees itself negated in God and sees God negated in itself."

"He who gives everything has everything or otherwise has nothing."

"Knowledge of my nothingness has given me the All."

"To think is of no use here, nor is to act, nor to speak. Love brings me to great heights. Thinking is no longer of any use here."

For further reading: Marguerite Porète. A Mirror for Simple Souls.

RABI' AL – ADAWIYYA

713–801. Sold as a slave, she was given her freedom by her master who discovered her praying surrounded by light. Mystical love and union with God are the themes that she develops. Long before the Sufis, she champions total union with the divine.

"What remains in this unity of you and me? And how can there be such a thing as a man or a woman?"

"What matters is to reach a higher level than the one in which we now find ourselves."

"It is not possible to distinguish with one's eyes the different stations of the path that leads to God nor it is possible with the tongue to reach Him. But awaken your heart. If your hearts awakens, then you will see with your own eyes the path and it will be easy to reach the station."

"I am going to Heaven to throw fire in paradise and to pour water onto hell. Thus neither will remain and what will appear will be that which is the goal. Then men will consider God without hope or fear and in that way they will adore him. For if there was no longer the hope of paradise or the fear of hell, would they not love the true with greater vigour?"

For further reading: Rabi'al: The Songs.

DJALAL-AL-DIN MUHAMMAD RUMI

1207–1273. One of the greatest Islamic mystical poets, Rumi studied in Damascus with Ibn Arabi, then with his teacher, Shams. He dedicated himself to meditation and to dance and founded the Mevlevi Order of whirling dervishes. He wrote the Mathnawi, an odyssey of the soul that must die to the ego in order to live eternally within God.

"I was snow. You melted me. The soil drank me. Mist of the spirit, I drift up to the sun."

"In the night of my heart along a narrow path I dug and the light sprang forth, an infinite land of light."

"Happy the moment when you are seated, you and me, different in form and face but having the same soul."

"God has made the non-existent appear as the magnificent existent and he has made the existent appear as the non-existent."

"From the moment that you came into the world of existence, a ladder was placed before you to allow you to escape. First you were mineral, then you became plant. Next you became an animal. How could you fail to understand? Then you became man with the gift of understanding, of reason, of faith. Consider what perfection this body drawn from dust has acquired. When you will have transcended the condition of man, then you will no doubt become an angel. When you have finished with earth, then your home will be heaven. You need to go beyond the angelic condition. Dive into the ocean so that your drop can become a sea."

Just like Angelus Silesius and Hinduism using the Leela, Rumi speaks to us of our potential evolution.

For further reading: The Mystic Odes of Rumi.

THE SECRET OF THE GOLDEN FLOWER

Lu Tzu, the author of The Secret of the Golden Flower, lived in the 8th century AD and is said to have been a distant disciple of Lao Tzu. The text is a practical Taoist treatise on how to crystallize the soul. Carl Jung wrote a commentary on it.

"Turning the light around is a way of concentrating the higher soul and thus of preserving the spirit. It is by this means that the lower soul is mastered."

"When one fixes thought on the central point between the eyes, the light shines out by itself. The act of fixing thought between one's eyes provokes the penetration of the light within."

"The disciple understands the means of distilling wholly the inferior dark soul so that it becomes pure light."

"One must move and fix the light. By doing so, you provoke the turning round of the light. After a while a new spiritual body is created."

"If man can make his heart die, the original spirit will awake to life. To make one's heart die does not mean to have it wither or discolor. It does mean though that it has become one without division."

For further reading: Thomas Cleary. The Secret of the Golden Flower.

SHANKARA

A spiritual master of the VIIIth century, Shankara brought about the renaissance of Hinduism. He proposed one key principle, Brahman, the Absolute, of which all other gods are but partial manifestations. He travelled throughout India teaching Advaita-Vedanta and founded a religious order that is still in existence today.

"To confuse Being with non-Being is the cause of man's enslavement. It is through this misconception, a child of ignorance, that the calamities of birth and death stem for man believes that he is this crude body whose days are numbered. He identifies with it and, in so doing, attaches himself to the body as closely as does the caterpillar to the cocoon."

"Realization occurs as soon as the student succeeds in discerning for sure the difference between the Self and the non-Self. You should therefore practise to recognize the individual soul and the eternal Self!"

"Water filled with impurities reassumes its original limpidity once the matter suspended in it has been eliminated. The Atman reveals itself in all its splendour as soon as one has eliminated that which seemed to soil it."

"When the unreal ceases to exist, one realizes that the individual soul is in fact the Eternal Self. It is therefore one's duty to separate the Eternal Self from all additions such as the sense of the ego and so on and so forth."

For further reading: Shankara. The Crest Jewel of Discrimination: how to discriminate the spectator from the spectacle.

SHANTIDEVA

Born in the VIIth century, Shantideva, the son of a king, renounced the throne and became a monk. He travelled throughout India, saving thousands from famine by multiplying the amounts of food available and accomplishing numerous miracles. His treatise 'Steps towards Enlightenment' is a summary of spiritual realization.

"He who wishes to abide by the rules must keep a careful control over his mind. The rule cannot be kept by anyone who does not keep his erratic spirit in check."

"When attention stands by the spirit's door in order to guard it, vigilance comes and, even if it retreats, comes back."

"I must first of all understand my state of mind and when at fault remain as sturdy as a stump."

"When neither reality nor non-reality come to mind, then, in the absence of all possible steps, the mind liberated from the thrall of concepts quietens down."

For further reading: Shantideva. Steps towards Enlightenment.

SUFISM

Sufism appears during the XIth century as a reaction to traditional Islamic vision and is a body of knowledge that liberates and opens onto the divine. Man is viewed as an exile. His life depends on his recognition of this exile and on his finding within himself

the means to return to his real nature.
Through the love of Allah (Rabia).

Through union with Allah because of man's essential identity with
him: "I am God." (Hallaj).

Through a non-dualistic approach leading to unitary consciousness (Ibn Arabi).

Through abstraction in which the succeeding concept erases the
former (Niffari).

Al Junayd: "The essence of Sufism lies in God making you die to
yourself in order to resurrect you in Him."

To die to one's self is 'fana', which means extinction.

THE DIAMOND SUTRA AND THE HEART SUTRA
The literal meaning of sutra is string or cord or narrative thread.
The sermons of the Buddha were transcribed as sutras which are
generally made up of short, incisive phrases.

The Heart and the Diamond are two of the forty sutras that form
the Prajnaparamita. These sutras are of great significance in the
Chan and Zen tradition for in them is stated the formulation of
the void. These sutras are famous throughout the Himalayan and
the Sino-Japanese worlds. They are recited and used in meditation
for their understanding of the void.

DIAMOND SUTRA
"Not being an object of consciousness, absolute reality is not
within reach of ordinary consciousness."

"A great Being should cultivate a mind that is free of all fixations,
he should cultivate a mind that freezes on nothing, he should
cultivate a mind that does not support itself on any form, on any
sounds, on any smell, on any taste nor on mental phenomena."

HEART SUTRA

"All things are empty: Nothing is born, nothing dies, nothing is pure, nothing is stained, nothing increases and nothing decreases."

"With nothing to attain, the Bodhisattva leans on transcendent knowledge and lodges there. Free from hindrance, no fears exist for apart from every perverted view the Bodhisattva dwells in nirvana."

JOHN TAULER

1300–1361. John Tauler was a Dominican monk about whom little is known except that he met Meister Eckhart. He is in the lineage of the Rhenish mystics.

"You are dispersed, full of images and God does not lie fully in your heart. In truth, the obstacle is not your outer endeavours, nor anything else, but you."

"If you wish to be macerated and digested by God, you must die to yourself and be rid of the old man for if food is to turn into the nature of man, it must necessarily lose its own nature."

"Be sure of this: If you wish to reach perfection, you will have to get rid of everything that is not God."

"To know the One in the All and the All in the One, what a magnificent invention! Only those who have reached that point know perfectly what is true joy."

"Above all convince yourself that you are nothing. For it is our pretention to be something that prevents God from fulfilling his great work in us."

"If you leave yourself completely, God will enter completely. The more you go out, the more he goes in, neither more no less."

"However noble, however pure images are, they are always a screen for the contour-less image that is God."

For further reading: John Tauler. The History and Life of the Reverend Doctor John Tauler of Strasbourg.

ECKHART TOLLE
Born 1948. Eckhart Tolle, a contemporary spiritual teacher. Speaks of his awakening as the death of the ego. Through his book 'The

Power of Now', he has conveyed an understanding of non-duality to millions of readers. He sees the ego as a pain-body.

"Thinking is only a small aspect of consciousness. Thought cannot exist without consciousness but consciousness does not need thought."

"When you start to disidentify and become the watcher, the pain-body will continue to operate for a while and will try to trick you into identifying with it again."

"Stay present, stay conscious. Be the ever-alert guardian of your inner space."

"Identification with the mind gives it more energy; observation of the mind withdraws energy from it. Identification with the mind creates more time; observation of the mind opens up the dimension of the timeless."

For further reading: Eckhart Tolle. The Power of Now.

THE UPANISHADS
The Upanishads are a metaphysical treatise. They are considered part of divine revelation, the shruti. As a whole they form the Vedanta, which is the culmination of the Vedas. They are at the historical heart of Hinduism and frequently appear as a teaching session between a teacher and a disciple. Shankara (see entry) wrote a commentary on them.

ISA UPANISHAD
Written some time between 800 and 500 BC, the Isa Upanishad is probably the first composed in verse.

"Into deep darkness fall those who follow the immanent. Into deeper darkness fall those who follow the transcendent."

"Reality is other than to those who follow action and other than to those who follow knowledge. This have we heard from the sages who explained this truth to us."

"He who knows both the transcendent and the immanent, with the immanent overcomes death and with the transcendent reaches immortality."

KENA UPANISHAD
"We gain an immortal state when we perceive it in each apprehension. We obtain the self via force. We gain knowledge through immortality."

"To possess knowledge in the world is truth. Not to own knowledge on earth is an immense loss. The sages apply discernment. They leave this world and become immortal."

KATHA UPANISHAD
"Awake! Arise! Strive for the highest and be in the light! Sages say the path is narrow and difficult to tread, narrow as the edge of a razor."

"What is beyond sound and form, without touch and taste and perfume, is eternal, unchangeable and without beginning or end, without reasoning. When that consciousness manifests, man becomes free from the jaws of death."

VEDANTA
Among the various Hindu schools of thought, Vedanta is the one most intimately linked with the Indian religion. Advaita Vedanta (non-dualism) is the main influence to have come out of Vedanta.

For Vedanta, material or mental phenomena exist only in relation to the ultimate reality, which is pure consciousness. It is both indestructible and autonomous. When an individual per-ceives a phenomenon from his point of view, this phenomenon supports his ego. When an individual perceives a phenomenon from reality's point of view, the relative reality of the phenomenon disappears as well as the ego which this perception underpins. The classic Vedantin example is that of the serpent and the rope. In a darkened room a man sees a serpent. Fear, panic, adrenaline and the desire for flight seize hold of him. Suddenly he realizes that what he took for a serpent is no more than a rope. The mental projection which nourished his ego collapses and if the man is mature, so does his ego.

VIJNANA BHAIRAVA

The Vijnana Bhairava was composed in the 6th century BC. This Kashmiri Shivaite manual provides techniques that point towards awakening. Its practice urges us to live our senses to the full. There is no break between the mystical and the worldly. Every thought, every emotion, if followed through to its origin, brings us to unity, to the divine.

"One must concentrate on the beginning or on the end of any phenomena. Through the power of the void become void, one will take the shape of the void."
Verse 40.

"All things manifest through the knowledge of the Self and the Self manifests through all things. As a result of the essence that they share, knowledge and known reveal themselves as one."
Verse 137.

"A stable and character-less mind, without origin, that in truth is what we call contemplation. But colorful visualizations of divinities endowed with bodies, organs, faces and hands have nothing in common with true contemplation." Verse 146.

VIMALAKIRTI

Vimalakirti is a contemporary of the Buddha. His teachings point towards man's fundamental freedom. He brings us to the limits of the world of form and to the void. His sutra of the Inconceivable Liberation was first translated in Chinese in the third century after Christ.

"That which is called awakening is not an entity which can be physically or spiritually seized."

"Awakening cannot be analysed as it is not subject to the slightest conditioning."

"Awakening is non-action as it has no relation to thought."

"Awakening is non-dual because it transcends spirit and things."

"Awakening takes up no space for it is not material and has no shape."
"Awakening cannot be seized for it tends towards no object."

"Awakening is an end in itself for one finds oneself at the summit of the real."

For further reading: Vimalakriti. The Holy Teachings of Vimalakriti.

WEI WU WEI
1895-1986. Wei Wu Wei, whose real name was Terence Gray, was a modern Ch'an master of Irish extraction. He travelled to India and was influenced by Ramana Maharshi. He developed a body of teachings based on Ch'an masters, within which he pushes concepts to their abstract limits so that the reader loses his grabbing points. He spent his final years in Monaco.

"Why are you unhappy?
Because 99.9 per cent
Of everything you think,
And of everything you do,
Is for yourself –
And there isn't one."

"When the dreamer awakens, he is absolute absence."

"To transcend pleasure and pain is achieved not by diving into the one or the other but by experiencing the inexistence of the one and of the other."

"There is no objective process which can lead to awakening as awakening is to wake out of a dream and the dream is a process of objectification in so far as to objectify is to continue to dream. Awakening consists in bringing this process to an abrupt end by ceasing to look in the wrong direction."

"Just as the eye cannot see itself, so truth cannot express itself because being non-dual, it cannot be transmitted in duality as the object of a subject."

"The integral mind has no thoughts for thoughts come from the divided mind."

"Truth is manifested when you know that you neither 'are' nor 'are not'. To get to know it, you do not need to see but to cease seeing for where there is no vision, it is."

For further reading: Wei Wu Wei. Ask the Awakened. The Negative Way.

KEN WILBER

Born 1949. Ken Wilber is an American philosopher who has elaborated a brilliant metaphysical synthesis which he names the Integral Theory. He sees ultimate reality as non-dual and forms that evolve in time are fundamentally nothing else but void.

"The great and rare mystics of the past (from Buddha to Christ, from al-Hallaj to Lady Tsogyal, from Hui-Neng to Hildegard) were, in fact, ahead of their time, and are still ahead of ours. In other words, they are not figures of the past. They are figures of the future."

"Evolution occurs in the world of time and space and form, whereas Spirit's primordial nature is finally timeless and Formless, prior to evolution but not other to it. We do not find Spirit or Emptiness by reaching some evolutionary Omega point in time, but rather by stepping off the cycle of time and evolution altogether."

"The Witness is a huge step forward, and it is a necessary and important step in meditation, but it is not ultimate. When the Witness or the soul is finally undone, then the Witness dissolves into everything that is witnessed. The subject/object duality collapses and there is only pure non-dual awareness."

For further reading: Ken Wilber. A Theory of Everything: An Integral Vision for Business, Politics, Science and Spirituality

A Letter from the Reader to Himself

My Dear Child,

Since blue-green algae, you have come a long way – vegetable, animal, human – and have not ceased to evolve. Your eternal consciousness has clothed itself in a multitude of envelopes. I have been waiting for you since time immemorial for you are nothing else but me. The illusion that surrounds you must separate us no more. You must now start on the journey and be ready to leave this planet. I cannot help you from the outside, for where I am inner and outer are One. In order for us to find each other, you must discover the truth for only it can save you. I cannot give it to you for it is my substance and I cannot divide myself. But I can tell you where to find it. For a long time you have searched for it outside yourself, whether in the depths of matter by creating particle accelerators or on the outer edges of space by sending telescopes in orbit. That is not where you will find it. It is not outside yourself. It lies at the very heart of your being. All you have to do is to want me passionately and follow the path of those who have already found me, and we will soon be reunited.

Your Consciousness that wants you to Get Out of this World Alive.

GLOSSARY

Awakening
Awakening is a generalized neural short-circuit triggered by the right question through which the psychological identity, the ego, is extinguished. It is the abolition of the mechanism that generates the subject-object dynamic. As a result the sense of being at one with all things arises.

Choice of least harm
The choice of least harm is the program through which our choices in life are made. It is a compromise established by the unconscious to strike a balance between the program whose task is to never let go of our identifications - a base program which is linked to fear and guilt; and the contradiction of having a surface program whose function is to move permanently towards the pleasant and to avoid the unpleasant. The choice of least harm lies at the root of the repetitive scenarios that punctuate our lives.

Consciousness
The consciousness that we know is linked to identification. It is a mental reflex-action linking subject and object. It is a system that maintains itself through its grabbing points. It is perfectly sum-marised by Descartes' Cogito, ergo sum (I think, therefore I am). The aim of the work on oneself is to shift from a consciousness that is identified and fragmented to a consciousness that is unified.

Conscious Ego or Witness
The part of us which deliberately identifies with sensory perceptions, then lets the mental film of our thoughts and feelings unfurl without judging or interfering. The conscious ego, or the witness, is the fruit of Distancing. (See entry)

Conscious Winning Choice
The program of the choice of least harm (see entry) disengaged from fear and guilt and under the guidance of a well-established directional ego. (See entry.)

Decoys or lures
Identifications, often irrational, produced by the ego to block consciousness in order to maintain grabbing points whenever

these are at risk. They are a key element in the ego's defence system. They fall into four categories. Firstly, when identified with thought, you judge, justify, or conclude. Then when you are identified with an emotion entirely alien to the situation. Then when you produce a mental fog which will diminish your intellectual sharpness, disconnecting your memory and, as a result, blocking your introspective abilities. Then, as a final defence, when you trigger a mystical experience producing a divine or a diabolic vision linked to your particular system of belief in order to keep the subject-object dynamic going.

Distancing
The ability to observe one's thoughts and feelings without judging, without drawing any conclusions.

Discernment
The questioning, digging, introspecting process by which we explore our unconscious mechanisms and gradually compel them to become conscious.

Disidentification
Disidentification is the key. To disidentify means to let go. It happens when we have a good practice of Distancing and when we have pushed Discernment deep and often enough into our repressed layers. It is when we disidentify that the directional ego of a seeker begins to be effective. It is then too that we dismantle the program of unconscious losing choices and move towards more conscious winning ones. At this stage the crystallization of the psychic body grows into the space that we have created in the old emotional body.

Discrimination
Discrimination is the ability to challenge yourself with questions linked to what you really are – ultimate reality, the Absolute, our true nature – and what you are not – your identifications, making up your psychological entity. Discrimination is the very heart of metaphysical inquiry.

Duality
The mechanism of identification between subject and object, maintained by sensory perceptions, emotions, memory and thoughts.

Directional Ego
The part of us that remains in control even when the other aspects of ourselves surge up and try to modify our perception of the situation. All the major qualities such as ethics, integrity, honesty spring from a directional ego. Success depends on the existence of a well-built directional ego that organizes life according to its own objectives.

Ego
The ego is made up of everything with which we have identified consciously and unconsciously. It is our psychological entity. It is the armour that protects our vulnerable child which is why it will do anything to hold onto its identifications. The aim of the ego is to grow endlessly. It is a nonentity, an illusion that maintains itself via the subject-object dynamic.

Emotional Body
We realize that we have an emotional body when we become conscious of physical sensations – for example in the throat, the solar plexus or the stomach. We can also be aware of its existence when we avoid certain situations such as a breakup in order not to experience physical pain. The dismantling of the emotional body creates space for the crystallization of the soul.

Grabbing point or Identification
Everything with which we identify is a grabbing point. We are constantly in identification with our senses, our thoughts, our emotions. Awakening occurs when we lose all our grabbing points in one go. The image that best illustrates the grabbing points is the Greek myth of the many-headed Hydra. Unless all the heads are cut off in one go, they grow again and again.

Guilt
Guilt is the concept that best defines the effects of identification with the primary fear linked to the pain of birth. Our psychological identity is built on this energy, on this identification. To maintain itself, guilt will create the suffering and the failure that we keep encountering in our life.

Metaphysical Inquiry
This is the process in which we challenge ourselves with existensial questions to which we do not have easy answers. This is the best way of forcing the burgeoning of new neural connections.

Non-dualism, non-duality
This defines the real, the Absolute, God, life beyond identifications. Non-dualism, also known as non-duality, is our true nature veiled by the subject-object dynamic that creates and maintains our apparent identity.

Practice of Silence
The practice of silence is highly recommended by all the spiritual traditions. It aims towards the absence of thought. Whenever you stabilize three sensorial fields into one, you are already practicing silence and opening yourself up to the development of the psychic body, the soul. This also improves your intuitive abilities.

Psychic body or soul
That part of us that is conscious independently of the physical body. The psychic body crystallizes within the physical body. The practice of silence and the dismantling of the psychological layers forming the shadow are the techniques by which this body can be developed. The psychic body can only evolve if the imagination is firmly mastered.

Seeker
The seeker is an aspect of our self made up of a desire to evolve and of an understanding of the mechanisms that rule us. The four qualities essential to its success are: awareness, discipline, courage and intellectual honesty.

Shadow
The shadow is everything that lies in the unconscious. The mechanisms of guilt and fear that drive us are to be found there. The psychological work of Distancing and Discernment consists in dismantling the shadow and in thus creating a directional ego that will be less subject to it.

Soul
See Psychic Body.

Subpersonalities
Repetitive mechanisms that associate perceptions, thoughts and emotions in a cohesive manner and supporting similar behavior patterns. A look, a smell, a desire will trigger off a thought, and then another. Biologically speaking, the same neural connections will self-perpetuate before reaching the hypothalamus. This will generate protein-modifying cells that will set off the same emotional flux. We are addicted to the mechanisms that constitute us.

Top of the skull or vertex
Focusing attention on the top of the skull, or the vertex, while practicing silence will allow one to feel these zones with greater sensitivity. This feeling will initially remind one of Distancing. In later stages, as Taoists and Buddhist paintings clearly show, it will be used as a gate by the psychic body.

Unconscious
The first task of the unconscious is to protect our vulnerable child. Much like a fortress protected by successive layers of defensive walls, it is made up of layers, each layer shielding the one below it. Repressed anger protects repressed fear that protects repressed guilt. To work on one's self means to become aware of the defence mechanisms of our unconscious and to dismantle them.

Unconscious Losing Choices
The program of the choice of least harm when linked to the logic of your shadow. (See also conscious winning choice).

Vulnerable Child
The shock of birth transforms the infant into the vulnerable child. This vulnerability has to be protected at all costs, and it is from this need that our grabbing points, our identifications, our personal identity arise.

Witness
See Conscious Ego.

BIBLIOGRAPHY

ESSENTIAL READING LIST

To read the texts is a vital part of the work. But the goal is neither to have a sophisticated understanding of reality, nor to be a scholar. The goal is to experience the upper levels of consciousness and, ultimately, awakening.

Limit yourself to a few books and understand them thoroughly. Do not read to reinforce your system of belief. Read to sharpen your questionings.

One final suggestion. If you find a book difficult, do not persist. In six months or a year, the book that you cannot get into now may well reveal its secrets.

Aldous Huxley
The Perennial Philosophy. HarperCollins.

Angelus Silesius
The Cherubinic Wanderer. Maria Shrady, Josef Schmidt, E. J. Furchaby. (Translator). Classics of Western Spirituality. (Paperback).

Astavakra Gita
Song of the Self Supreme. Motilal Banarsidass.

Huang Po
The Zen Teachings of Huang Po on the Transmission of Mind, ed. John Blofeld. Grove Press. Bibliography

Nisargadatta Maharaj
I Am That. Acorn Press and Kalpataru Books.
Pointers from Nisargadatta Maharaj. Ramesh Balsekar. Acorn Press.

Irina Tweedie
The Chasm of Fire. Element Books.

The Gospel according to Thomas
The Gospel according to Thomas. Trans. Marvyn Meyer. HarperSanFrancisco.
www.humanityunitedforum.com/en_the_gospel_of_thomas.pdf

The Secret of the Golden Flower
Thomas Cleary. HarperOne. HarperCollins.

Wei Wu Wei
Ask the Awakened: The Negative Way. Sentient Publications.
All Else is Bondage. Non-Volitional Living. Hong Kong University
Press and Midpoint Trade Books.

RECOMMENDED READING LIST

Al-Junayd
Life, personality and writings of Al Junayd. Ali Hassan Abdel. Gibb
Memorial Trust.

Avadhut Gita
Mahatma Dattatreya
Publisher: José J. de Olañeta

Bhagavad Gita
Simon Brodbeck (Introduction), Juan Mascaro (Translator). Penguin
Books Ltd.

Jacob Böhme
Jacob Böhme. Essential Readings. HarperCollins.
The Keys of Jacob Böhme. Phanes Press.

Buddhism
Radiant Mind, Essential Buddhist Teachings and Texts. ed. Jean Smith.
Riverhead Books.
The Foundations of Buddhism. Rupert Gethin. Oxford Paperbacks.

Ch'an or Zen
www.selfdiscoveryportal.com

Deepak Chopra
Life After Death: The Book of Answers. Rider & Co.

The Heart Sutra
Essence of the Heart Sutra: The Dalai Lama's Heart of Wisdom.
Teachings. Bstan-Dzin-Rgya-Mtsho et al. Wisdom Pub.

A Translation of the Heart Sutra. Douglas Fox. Edwin Mellen Press. The Diamond Sutra.

Dalai Lama
The Art of Happiness: A Handbook for Living by His Holiness the Dalai Lama and Howard Cutler. Publisher: Mobius.

Freud
On Melancholy. Manuscript G addressed to Wilhelm Fliess. January 1895.

Gurdjieff
In Search of the Miraculous, Fragments of an Unknown Teaching. P.D. Ouspenski. Harvest Books.
Quotations from G.I. Gurdjieff's Teaching. G.I. Gurdjieff. Luzac Oriental.

Hadewijch of Antwerp
Hadewijch: The Complete Works. Classics of Western Spirituality. ed Mother Columba Hart. Paulist Press.

Hallaj
The Tawasin of Mansur al-Hallaj. Diwan Press.

Hsin Hsin Ming
Verses on the Faith Mind by Chien-chih Seng-ts'an Third Zen Patriarch. Web Publication by Mountain Man Graphics, Australia. Southern Summer 1997.

Ibn Arabi
The Mysteries of Bearing Witness to the Oneness of God and the Prophethood of Ibn-Al-Arabi. The Bezels of Wisdom. Classics of Western Spirituality Series. R. W. Austin (Editor). Titus Burckhardt-Con.

Muhammad
The Koran. Great Books of the Islamic World.
The Koran. N.J. Dawood (Translator). Penguin Classics.

Isa, Kena, Katha Upanishad.
The Upanishads. Juan Mascaro (Translator). Penguin Classics.

Jesus
The New Testament.
Trans. Marvyn Meyer. HarperSanFrancisco.

Jung
Memories, Dreams, Reflections. C.G. Jung. Fontana Press.
Modern Man in Search of a Soul. C.G. Jung. Routledge.

Krishnamurti
Krishnamurti's Notebook. Jiddu Krishnamurti.
Krishnamurti Publications of America.
On Love and Loneliness. J. Krishnamurti.
Krishnamurti Publications of America.
On Living and Dying. J. Krishnamurti.
Krishnamurti Publications of America.

Kabbalah
The Ladder of Lights. William G. Gray. Red Wheel. Weiser.
The Garden of Pomegranates. Israel Regardie. Llewellyn Publications.

Lalla Ded
The Wise Sayings of Lal-Ded – A Mystic Poetess of Ancient Kashmir.
K.C.I.E Sir George Grierson. Obscure Press.

Lao Tzu
Tao Te Ching. Lao Tzu. D. C. Lau (Translator). Penguin Books.

Lieh-Tzu
A Taoist Guide to Practical Living. Shambhala.

Lin-Chi
The Zen Teachings of Master Lin-Chi. Burton Watson. Columbia University Press.

Ramana Maharshi
Talks with Sri Ramana Maharshi. Kalpataru Books.
Ramana Maharshi Website & www.sentient.org
The Essential Teachings of Ramana Maharshi: A Visual Journey.
Matthew Greenblatt (Editor). InnerDirections Publishing.

Talks With Ramana Maharshi. On Realizing Abiding Peace and Happiness.
Inner Directions Foundation.

Marcus Aurelius
The Meditations of Marcus Aurelius: Spiritual Teachings and Reflections. Sacred Wisdom. Watkins.

Robert Augustus Masters
Spiritual Bypassing: When Spirituality Disconnects Us from What Really Matters, North Atlantic Books, Berkeley, California.

Meister Eckhart
Meister Eckhart. Oliver Davies (Translator). Penguin Books.

Niffari
The Mawaqif and Mukhatabat of Muhammad ibn Abd-al-Jabbar al-Hasan al-Niffari with other fragments. Arthur John Arberry. Gibb Memorial Trust.

Plato
The Symposium. Plato. Walter Hamilton (Translator), Christopher Gill. Penguin Books.

Plotinus
The Enneads. John Dillon (Introduction), Stephen MacKenna (Translator). Penguin Classics.

Marguerite Porète
The Mirror of Simple Souls. Marguerite Porète. Ellen Babinsky (Translator). Paulist Press.

Rabbi Nachman
The Tales of Rabbi Nachman, Martin Buber.
Prometheus Books UK.
Mysticism and Madness: The Religious Thought of Rabbi Nachman of Bratslav.
Robert & Arlene Kogod Library of Judaic Studies. Continuum International Publishing Group Ltd.

Rabia
The Oxford Book of Mystical Verse. Oxford University Press.
First Among Sufis, The Life and Thoughts of Rabia al-Adawyya. Octagon Press.
The Sayings of Rabia. Doorkeeper of the Heart version of Rabia. Trans. Charles Upton Putney. Threshold Books.
www.sufimaster.org/adawyya

Rumi
The Essential Rumi. Selected Poems. Jalal al-din Rumi. Penguin Classics.

Shankara
The Crest Jewel of Discrimination: Swami Prabhavandana and Christopher Isherwood. Vedanta Press and Bookshop.

Shantideva
The Way of Bodhisattva. Padmakara Translation Group. Shambhala Publications.

The Gospel according to Thomas
The Gospel according to Thomas. Trans. Mervyn Meyer. Harper San Francisco.

Vijnana Bhairava Tantra: The Ascent
by Satyasangananda Saraswati
http://www.upnaway.com/~bindu/anantayoga
web/vijnanabhairava/vijnanabhairava.html

John Tauler
The History and Life of the Reverend Doctor John Tauler of Strasbourg BiblioBazaar.
The History and Life of the Reverend Doctor John Tauler of Strasbourg with Twenty-Five of His Sermons.

Eckhart Tolle
The Power of Now. Hodder Mobius.

Vimalakirti
The Holy Teachings of Vimalakriti. ed Robert A. F. Thurman. Penn State Press.

Wei Wu Wei
Ask the Awakened: The Negative Way.
All Else is Bondage.
Open Secret.
The Tenth Man.
Reflections of a Pilgrim on the Way.
Why Lazarus Laughed.
Sentient Publications.
Open Secret. Hong Kong University Publications.
The Tenth Man: The Great Joke Which Made Lazarus Laugh.
Sentient Publications.
Unworldly Wise: As the Owl Remarked to the Rabbit. Hong Kong University Publications.

APHORISMS

"Who am I?" is the key that opens the door to success.

The body wants to go on and on. The ego does not want to let go of its identifications. The soul wants to evolve. Your true nature does not want anything: it simply is.

Just as a thought cannot think, a perception cannot perceive. Everything that you know belongs to the nature of what is perceived. Can what is perceived perceive?

When your true nature reveals itself to itself, you realize that you have always been everything.

Your true nature is unreachable. As long as you perceive differences, you are a stranger to what you really are.

Grace is an effect without a cause.

By getting rid of tomorrow you weaken fear. By weakening fear you diminish your inner tyrant.

What is repressed always comes back to bite you.

You need to see what you do not want to see in yourself.

To open your heart you must ride your fears.

Love is the gift of one's self that comes from self-forgetting.

A truly evolved soul knows that what is never becomes and that what becomes never is. It therefore lets go of becoming to be absorbed by being.

Man's true worth lies in his decision to go beyond his condition, which is always the result of his belief system.

What you call God is nothing but life tasting itself in a total absence of conditioning.

The ego, the individual, the psychological entity is no more than the defence system of your vulnerable child.

Awakening, like death, is just the end of mental habits and the end of mental habits is just like the end of a dream.

The psychological structure is made up of layers. Digging into these layers is the very essence of the work on one's self.

To understand identification leads to disidentification. And the space opened up by disidentification is the cradle of the soul.

Dictatorship is to a people what the ego is to what you are, so overthrow its tyranny.

Consciousness decides, the unconscious executes. All you need is to be aligned.

Winning choices are recognised not through your intellect but through sensation.

WEBSITE

http://www.AlainForget.com